Run to the City

Abundant Living After the Well

By:

Laurie Nave

Copyright © 2022 by Singing River Publishing

All rights reserved. No part of this publication may be reproduced, distributed, or transmitted in any form or by any means, including photocopying, recording, or other electronic or mechanical methods, without the prior written permission of the publisher, except in the case of brief quotations embodied in critical reviews and certain other noncommercial uses permitted by copyright law. For permission requests, write to the author, addressed "Attention: Permissions " at
https://www.singingriverpublishing.com

Cover Illustration by: Tia Davis

SINGING RIVER PUBLISHING

Florence, Alabama

www.singingriverpublishing.com

First Edition

Acknowledgements

I would like to thank my wonderful husband, Larry for his love, support, and encouragement. He truly loves me as Christ loved the church.

I am so thankful for my parents, both of whom loved me and raised me in the "nurture and admonition of the Lord." They lived as examples of faithful believers, loving spouses, and consistent, attentive parents.

I am so thankful for the people who have impacted my life and taught me how to study God's Word, pray without ceasing, and serve Christ. From my youth minister and his wife, to fellow students in college and beyond, to faithful, long-time friends who - like Jesus does - have loved me through thick and thin and have exemplified what redemption looks like.

And most of all, I am thankful to the Lord Jesus Christ, who knew no sin, for becoming sin for us so that we can become the righteousness of God. Thank you, Lord, for saving me, sustaining me, casting my sin as far as the east is from the west, and using me even as I am broken.

Table of Contents

Introduction	1
Chapter 1	7
Chapter 2	15
Chapter 3	21
Chapter 4	33
Chapter 5	45
Chapter 6	55
Chapter 7	61
Chapter 8	81
Chapter 9	89
Chapter 10	103
Chapter 11	117
About the Author	125

Introduction

What happens after we fail? After we fall? After the confession and repentance before God? What then? What next? What does God say a believer should do after they turn from a life or a season of rebellion against Him? What if the sin was public, embarrassing, or hurtful? What does the Bible say about our service *after* we've spectacularly blown it?

In John 4, Jesus has an encounter with an unnamed woman simply known as a Samaritan woman. In church-ese, she is commonly known as, "The Woman at the Well." If you've not heard or read this story, you can read it below.

> "A woman of Samaria came to draw water. Jesus said to her, 'Give Me a drink.' For His disciples had gone away to the city to buy food. So the Samaritan woman said to Him, 'How is it that You, though You are a Jew, are asking me for a drink, though I am a Samaritan woman?' (For Jews do not associate with Samaritans.) Jesus replied to her, 'If you knew the gift of God, and who it is who is saying to you, "Give Me a drink," you would have asked Him, and He would have given you living water.' She said to Him, 'Sir, You have no bucket and the well is deep; where then

do You get this living water? You are not greater than our father Jacob, are You, who gave us the well and drank of it himself, and his sons and his cattle?' Jesus answered and said to her, 'Everyone who drinks of this water will be thirsty again; but whoever drinks of the water that I will give him shall never be thirsty; but the water that I will give him will become in him a fountain of water springing up to eternal life.'

"The woman said to Him, 'Sir, give me this water so that I will not be thirsty, nor come all the way here to draw water.' He said to her, 'Go, call your husband and come here.' The woman answered and said to Him, 'I have no husband.' Jesus said to her, 'You have correctly said, "I have no husband"; for you have had five husbands, and the one whom you now have is not your husband; this which you have said is true.' The woman said to Him, 'Sir, I perceive that You are a prophet. Our fathers worshiped on this mountain, and yet you Jews say that in Jerusalem is the place where one must worship.' Jesus said to her, 'Believe Me, woman, that a time is coming when you will worship the Father neither on this mountain nor in Jerusalem. You Samaritans worship what you do not know; we worship what we do know, because salvation is from the Jews. But a time is coming, and even now has arrived, when the true worshipers will worship the Father in spirit and truth; for such people the Father seeks to be His worshipers. God is spirit, and those who worship Him must worship in spirit and truth.' The woman said to Him, 'I know that Messiah is coming (He who is called Christ); when that One comes, He will declare all things to us.' Jesus said to her, 'I am He, the One speaking to you.'

"And at this point His disciples came, and they were amazed that He had been speaking with a woman, yet no one said, 'What are You seeking?' or, 'Why are You speaking with her?' So the woman left her waterpot and went into the city, and said to the people, 'Come, see a man who told me all the things that I have done; this is not the Christ, is He?' They left the city and were coming to Him." John 4:7-30

I've heard a lot of sermons and Sunday School lessons about this passage. I've heard sermons about racism, as the woman was a Samaritan and the Jews of that time despised Samaritans. Preachers and teachers have highlighted love transcending social conventions when Jesus asked a woman for a drink and talked to her alone. I've heard about the pain and loneliness of gossip and judgment, since she likely went to draw water in the heat of the day to avoid the other women and their stares.

And then there's the main theme of this encounter—salvation, conversion, and redemption—a fallen sinner's life-changing meeting with the Living Water. Water that will forever quench that inner thirst. That, and of course, evangelism. She left her water jar and ran to the city to tell others. That last part, in verses 28-30, has always intrigued me, and I wish the story didn't end there. I want to know more.

I've always wondered...what happened *after* the well? What happened after the woman's dramatic run back into town, when her declaration made people curious about this Jesus who was hanging around the water source? It says, "They left the city and were coming to Him," but what happened next? Did they see her differently? Did anyone dismiss her because of who she had been? After all, we humans are often guilty of judging the message by the messenger.

I wonder if, after that day, the woman began drawing water at the beginning and end of the day as the other women did. Did the townspeople ask her more questions? Did the ladies continue to gossip, or did they see the change in her life? Was she as confident in sharing her transformation a week later, a year later? How did the townspeople, especially the more "pious" ones, perceive and respond to her? After all, they knew what she had done. They knew how many husbands she'd had. They knew *her*.

They didn't know her as well as Jesus did. But I wonder if she had trouble remembering that in her day-to-day life. I have wondered if she struggled with shame and regret or if she was able to fully "leave her water jar." After all, her own heart had changed instantly; her surroundings, her history, and her reputation didn't. Just like us, her transformation was spiritual, but she still lived in the physical reality of her life.

That is why I am writing this. I know that woman because I am that woman. I have been her. No, I have not been married five times. But I have fallen and chosen sin, and more than a few of those choices were in full Technicolor. I have avoided going to the well at the usual times so I wouldn't have to face the gossip or my own problems.

I haven't just been the woman at the well. I've been Sarah, who took matters into her own hands when God wasn't moving fast enough. I've been David, wanting and taking what was not mine and then making things infinitely worse by trying to hide it. I've been Jacob, using deception to get what I needed. In short, I "have sinned and fallen short of the glory of God" (Romans 3:23) in ways that were worse than the typical Sunday School confessions of coveting a neighbor's nice heels.

Like each of these people, I had to come face to face with the truth and have had to choose repentance and brokenness. As He does, Jesus forgave and cleansed me through the utterly sufficient power of His redemptive work on the cross. He cleansed me from all unrighteousness. He separated my sin "as far as the east is from the west" (Psalm 103:12). He blotted out my transgressions and "remembers them no more" (Isaiah 43:25)

However, the facts of my past didn't change. The pain I caused to others didn't disappear. There was no *Men in Black* magical memory wipe. I still had to live in a community where everyone knew me. Honestly? It left me daunted. Every time I felt prompted to serve God in some way, to have Him use the gifts He has given me, questions plagued me:

Can I? After all my failings? I mean, I know He forgives and cleanses, but is there a point at which—even forgiven—someone has just been too bad to be useful to God? Was part of my "penance" for such egregious sins being relegated to the backroom, the shelf where we place tools that we don't want to toss but that are just too damaged to be useful? What was *I* supposed to do after the well?

I kept thinking about that woman. She didn't hesitate, she didn't overthink, she didn't flinch. She ran—*ran*—back to the town that held all her failures and rejections, all the gossip and judgment. She ran toward that city and told everyone she saw about what had happened during her encounter with Jesus.

As I wrestled with the questions that caused me to hesitate where she didn't, I realized she wasn't alone in God's Word. When Rahab hid the spies, she was bold enough to ask for protection for her household, and she didn't shrink back from the Israelites after the walls fell. She ended up marrying an Israelite and being one of only two women listed in Jesus' lineage.

Even after the terrible plan with Hagar and her husband that has lasting repercussions even today, Sarah gave birth to Isaac, and she became the matriarch of many nations. Her son became the father of Jacob, who fathered the twelve tribes of Israel. She's listed in Hebrews 11's "Hall of Faith."

Mary Magdalene followed Jesus and wasn't afraid or ashamed to wash His feet and dry them with her hair. Jonah ran away to avoid obedience, and God still used him to redeem Nineveh. Peter denied Jesus three times while the officials were deciding whether to crucify him. And yet on the Day of Pentecost, God used him to bring countless people to faith. Paul sought the early Christians and stood by while they were killed. After the road to Damascus, he went to those same early Christians to join them in the gospel.

The answer to what comes after the well is clear, even though the path might seem overwhelming, and we may feel especially unworthy. When He redeems, even if it's for the 100th time, He frees us to serve. He expects us to go. The Great Commission is for all of us.

You may say to yourself: *Laurie, you don't know what I have done! I've been terrible, and everybody knows! And I have been a Christian for years! How could I fall so badly? Who would want to hear from me now?*

You're right. I don't know the specifics of your life, and you don't know the specifics of mine. But I know Jesus. I know the Father. I know that He died on the cross, I know that His grace is sufficient, and I know His promises. I don't say "God wants to use you after the well" because it feels better. I say it because it is detailed over and over and ***over*** in His Word. From Eve, to David, to the disciples, God uses imperfect people.

The purpose of this book is to dive deep into God's Word to remind us to run to the city and to show us not just how to get there, but how to stay there.

Now, put down your water jar, and let's run together.

Chapter 1: Some Essential Questions

As I mentioned in the introduction, any time I felt called to serve I was plagued with questions about my qualifications to do so. There's nothing wrong with questions, as long as we are asking the right ones. I was asking the wrong questions, and until I asked and answered the right ones, I was going to be stuck.

There are some essential questions you need to ask as you're standing at that well, fresh from redemption by the Living Water. I want you to take a few minutes to think about these questions. How would you answer them? How does Jesus answer them?

1. How much of my sin debt did Jesus pay on the cross?
2. How complete is His forgiveness of our sin?
3. Who can snatch me out of God's hand?
4. What is it that makes us righteous or worthy?
5. How does God say we are to comfort others?

You probably have two sets of answers to those questions, especially if you grew up in church. The first set of answers is the expected set - the ones you learned in church or assume you *should* know. Of course, God forgives. Of course, Jesus paid it all. Of course, He is enough. These answers may come automatically. But sometimes not having the prescribed answers handy is an advantage. Reciting Sunday School answers on autopilot can keep us from really digging into our own hearts. After all, knowing in our minds isn't the same as truly knowing in our hearts.

The other often more honest answers are the ones underneath. The ones that quietly whisper to us or berate us as we try to sleep. They might be the more honest ones. This is where our fear and shame live. These are the questions that rattle us. Have we gone too far? Do we even have a "right" to be used by God anymore? Who would believe us anyway after all we did? Those redemption stories worked in the Bible, but in this age of cell phones and social media, there are limits, right? God can't overcome the internet gossip mill.

I'll answer that last bit with a verse I love: "Jesus is the same yesterday, today, and forever." Hebrews 13:8

The answers to those questions haven't changed, and they never will. That is why I can share the upcoming answers with confidence. Jesus answers those questions, and *He* never changes. "His Word is settled in Heaven forever" (Psalm 119:89)

How much of my sin debt did Jesus Pay?

My husband was paying off a credit card a few years ago, and he had a regular monthly amount that was automatically debited from his bank account every month. He kept good records, and each month the payment came out like clockwork. Once the last payment date passed, he looked forward to that letter from the credit card company, telling him the debt was paid in full. He waited a month, then two. By the third month, he was getting a bit annoyed. He'd paid the debt months ago and had still not received that letter.

So he called the company. He found out that he had a balance of 0.17. Seventeen cents! He had assumed that surely they would go ahead and add that 17 cents to his last payment. But they didn't. He still had a balance. He put the 17 cents on his debit card and, sure enough, within a couple of weeks the letter came. He had finally paid the debt.

Jesus doesn't work that way. When He became "obedient to the point of death on the cross" (Phil. 2:8), He paid the debt in full. There is nothing left over. Here are a few verses that confirm Jesus' full payment on the cross:

"Much more then, having now been justified by His blood, we shall be saved from the wrath of God through Him." Romans 5:9

"He made Him who knew no sin to be sin on our behalf, so that we might become the righteousness of God in Him." I Corinthians 5:21

"And when you were dead in your wrongdoings and the uncircumcision of your flesh, He made you alive together with Him, having forgiven us all our wrongdoings, having canceled the certificate of debt consisting of decrees against us, which was hostile to us; and He has taken it out of the way, having nailed it to the cross." Colossians 2:13-14

"Knowing that you were not redeemed with perishable things like silver or gold from your futile way of life inherited from your forefathers, but with precious blood, as of a lamb unblemished and spotless, the blood of Christ." I Peter 1:18-19

Jesus became the propitiation for our sins. Propitiation means He took all of our punishment. He was our substitute. There is no outstanding debt, no sneaky 17 cents waiting to be called into account. When Jesus said, "It is finished," He meant it.

How complete is His forgiveness for our sins?

"Forgive and forget." I'm not sure how those two words ever became joined. We all know those are two distinctly different things. When someone hurts us, we can forgive. Even if the hurt is heartbreaking, we can - with God's help - forgive them. But forgetting? Memory is something we cannot control. So regardless of the aforementioned phrase, forgiving and forgetting do not go together.

But for God, the Author of all, things are different. Let's take a look at a few verses about the way God forgives us:

"You forgave the guilt of Your people;
You covered all their sin. Selah
You withdrew all Your fury;
You turned away from Your burning anger."
Psalm 85:2-3

"'For they will all know Me, from the least of them to the greatest of them,' declares the Lord, 'for I will forgive their wrongdoing, and their sin I will no longer remember.' Jeremiah 31:34b. (I encourage you to read this entire chapter to see the completeness of God's forgiveness of His people, even after they spent years completely ignoring His warnings and His prophet.)

"If we confess our sins, He is faithful and righteous, so that He will forgive us our sins and cleanse us from all unrighteousness." I John 1:9

"As far as the east is from the west,
So far has He removed our wrongdoings from us." Psalm 103:12

A few years ago, I needed to whiten something that was not only faded, it was riddled with brown and yellow age spots. I bought a little bucket of OxyClean. I had seen the commercial where someone dips old, yellowed lace into a bowl of the product, and it comes out pure white. The enthusiastic spokesperson assured me that all my whites would be bright. I'll admit, the Oxy Clean made a pretty significant difference. But when I looked closely, I could still see traces of those age spots. The product was good, but it couldn't erase every trace of time and use.

Jesus? He doesn't leave behind any traces. When He cleanses you, as 1 John 1:9 says, He cleanses us from ALL unrighteousness. Isaiah 1:18 gives us the clearest picture: "...though your sins are as scarlet, they shall be as white as snow; though they are red like crimson, they shall be as wool." *(NASB)* He doesn't just brighten the faded, dingy white. He removes the deepest stain of sin.

Hebrews 10:17 tells us, like Jeremiah did, that our sins and lawless deeds "I will remember no more." This doesn't mean God is afflicted with some kind of divine amnesia. It means He makes the conscious choice to eliminate it from your account, to erase it from the ledger. So if someone says, "God, I need a list of all the sins you are holding against Laurie," God's answer would be: "Zero."

I like to imagine going to God over shame and self-condemnation about my past sin that I have already confessed and repented of, and having the Lord look at me and say, "What are you talking about? Your account is clear. It is all gone."

God's forgiveness is complete. Unlike us, He doesn't wait until we slip up again and then pull out a list of everything we have done wrong to berate us with, reminding us of all our failures. If a voice is continually reminding you of your past, already forgiven by the God of eternity...it is not God's voice who is speaking.

Who can snatch me out of God's hand?

Jesus addresses the answer to this question head-on in John 10:28-30:

"And I give them eternal life, and they will never perish; and no one will snatch them out of My hand. My Father, who has given them to Me, is greater than all; and no one is able to snatch them out of the Father's hand. I and the Father are one." NASB

Ephesians 4:30 tells us that we are "sealed by the Holy Spirit unto the day of redemption." Specifically, we are sealed with the Holy Spirit, who guarantees our inheritance. When God guarantees something, it's a sure thing. When we give our lives to Christ, and place our faith in His complete work on the cross, we are His. Jesus tells us no one can snatch us out of His hand, then He ups the ante, assuring us that no one is able to snatch us out of His Father's hand either.

"This is the essential, necessary truth of salvation by grace through faith as the gift of God" (Ephesians 2:8-9). We cannot acquire salvation that is dependent on Christ through our own efforts. If we do not have the power to earn salvation, we also do not have the power to lose it. God is the author and sustainer of our salvation.

What is it that makes us righteous or worthy?

This is a key question. Now, we know that God expects obedience. Jesus said that if we love Him we will keep His commandments (John 14:23). That means all of them. But is that actually what makes us righteous - what classifies us as righteous before a holy God?

No, it isn't. Our works are to be the result of being made righteous, but they do not create righteousness within us. Only Jesus can do that, as evidenced by the verses below:

"He made Him who knew no sin to be sin on our behalf, so that we might become the righteousness of God in Him." I Corinthians 5:21, NASB

"Looking for the blessed hope and the appearing of the glory of our great God and Savior, Christ Jesus, who gave Himself for us to redeem us from every lawless deed, and to purify for Himself a people for His own possession, eager for good deeds." Titus 2:13-14, NASB

"For Christ also suffered for sins once for all time, the just for the unjust, so that He might bring us to God, having been put to death in the flesh, but made alive in the spirit."
I Peter 3:18, NASB

Isaiah 64:6 tells us that *our* righteousness is as filthy rags. So if being considered righteous is up to us, we are most unfortunate. But when we confess, repent, and turn fully toward Christ, His righteousness covers us. We become the righteousness of God. It's hard to imagine, but it's glorious. We do not ever have to be ashamed in God's presence as believers because when God sees us, He sees His Son's righteousness.

How does God say we are to comfort others?

When we are doubting, telling ourselves that our failings disqualify us from being used by God, we are overlooking a verse that has become one of my favorites:

"Blessed be the God and Father of our Lord Jesus Christ, the Father of mercies and God of all comfort, who comforts us in all our affliction so that we will be able to comfort those who are in any affliction with the comfort with which we ourselves are comforted by God." II Corinthians 1:3-4, NASB

If we hide in the shame of our past, we may well be denying hope to someone who needs to hear our story. The principle of helping others who are traveling the same road we have traveled is universal. Organizations like Alcoholics Anonymous, grief support groups, and even Weight Watchers understand this principle and the importance of that "connection of like experience." Even Mary, Jesus's mother, understood this as she commiserated with Elizabeth about their upcoming miraculous births.

Have you ever been a part of one of those drive-through chains, the kind where someone pays for the person behind them, and then that person pays for the person behind *them*, and so on? We call it "paying it forward." Jesus is the ultimate example of that attitude. He gives us the ultimate comfort specific to our pain, even if it is self-inflicted. Imagine the person sitting in Sunday school, heavy with shame. If they see that God has restored you and me and that we can still be used to bring Him glory, what comfort and hope that could be to them!

God uses us. That was Jesus's plan from the beginning when He poured His life into those twelve regular, fallible men. They weren't perfect. In fact, Peter seemed to stumble more than the others. But look at how God used Him in Acts. Look at the words of First and Second Peter.

In truth, when you look at all of the questions asked in this chapter, the underlying question is this: *Is Jesus enough? Is He big enough? Is His grace enough? Is His righteousness enough?*

And the answer to those questions is a resounding yes.

Words from the Living Water

1. Several verses answer the essential question, "How much of my sin debt did Jesus pay?" Which of the verses listed spoke to your heart? How can you meditate on that verse this week to remind yourself of His perfect redemption?

2. Many times, when we make destructive or sinful choices, the enemy likes to whisper, "You aren't really His child. He has given up on you. There's no way He will keep you after this…" How can we point to God's Word to refute these whispers?

3. I Corinthians 5:21 says that when we repent and place our faith in Christ's finished work, we become "the righteousness of God." What does that mean to you? How does that manifest itself in your life?

Chapter 2: The Comfort of Conviction

"For whom the Lord loves He disciplines, and He punishes every son whom he accepts. It is for discipline you endure; God deals with you as sons; for what son is there whom his father does not discipline? But if you are without discipline, of which all have become partakers, then you are illegitimate children and not sons." Hebrews 12:6-8

The Kroger parking lot will always hold painful, yet comforting memories. For those who aren't southern, Kroger is a popular grocery store chain. It was also the site of my brokenness over months of sin and rebellion. That parking space about two-thirds of the way back was where I parked my car, turned on some music, and sobbed those "heaving sobs" dramatic novels describe.

In the weeks before that day, I rode a terrible emotional roller coaster. My mood was so unpredictable I went to the doctor. A well-meaning physician's assistant had me fill out a couple of rating scale questionnaires and declared my diagnosis to be bipolar disorder. In truth, my disorder was much less complex. I was guilty of sinning against my Father, and the conviction I felt and denial I persisted in was soul-crushing. I was running from the Holy Spirit, and I was exhausted.

But it was also a comfort once I realized how fervently God pursued me. His dogged intervention through sleepless nights, His

Word echoing in my head, and those whispers in the quiet were all reminders that I was His child. Just like the verses listed in the opening of this chapter say, God chastens his children because He loves us.

When we belong to Christ, and we turn away from Him in sin and disobedience, He pursues and convicts. He loves His children more than any parents have ever loved. Like the love of a truly caring parent, that love has boundaries. We've created a shamefully shallow definition of love in our society. We think love means unconditional acceptance and agreement with whatever someone decides and however they choose to live. But anyone who has raised a child understands the danger of that passive brand of so-called love. God's love is universal, His approval is not. Real love will not approve of what is spiritually harmful.

We can become awfully offended at God's limits. Like the child who wants to touch the pretty red coils of a stove or eat the colorful capsules in a medicine bottle, we think the word "no" is intended to spoil our fun. In reality, when God says "Thou shalt not," He is really saying to us, "Don't hurt yourself."

I learned the truth of that statement several times during my life. That day at Kroger, I was in incredible pain as a result of my choices. And what's more, I hurt other people whom I claimed to love. The weight of that conviction and understanding was excruciating. You may know what that feels like. The memory of that pain may still cause an ache you just can't seem to soothe. The weight of it feels crushing at times. God's conviction may feel like a humiliation.

As strange as it sounds, that pain you feel over your wrong choices means that God loves you enough to convict and chasten you. God cares so much about you, His precious child, He will do all He can to pull you back from that hot stove. And if you stubbornly reach out and touch it anyway, He will allow you to feel the pain.

But he's also there to heal. When we respond to His conviction with repentance, and we return to Him, we find love and forgiveness from the Father. Everything He does (even when it is painful) is because He loves His children with an everlasting love.

When you read farther in Hebrews, to chapter 12, you'll find these verses:

"For the moment, all discipline seems not to be pleasant, but painful; yet to those who have been trained by it, afterward, it yields the peaceful fruit of righteousness." Hebrews 12:11, NASB

Remember, in the first chapter of this book, we learned that Christ died for us so that we might become "the righteousness of God." The fruit of that righteousness is the obedience we live out each day. It is also the change that He creates in us, even the changes that come when we confess our sin. The change that can come from God's discipline. This is what Jesus means in Matthew 3:8 when He says to "bear fruit in keeping with repentance."

Hebrews 12 doesn't stop at verse 11. Verse 12 tells us:

"Strengthen the hands that are weak and the knees that are feeble, and make straight paths for your feet, so that the limb which is impaired may not be dislocated, but rather healed." NASB

Sound familiar? When God heals our pain - even the pain that is self-inflicted - He wants us to bear fruit by in turn coming alongside others who are walking the painful path we have walked.

When we belong to Christ, He convicts us, chastens us, and restores us. Then He expects us to continue to serve Him. Conviction is a comfort. It identifies us as His, and it means He is not done with us. He wants us to return to Him so that we can bear the fruit of righteousness.

If you cannot let go of the pain, take stock. Is God convicting your heart? If so, how would He want you to respond? And if you are debilitated, hurting over the sin you have already confessed, go back and read Hebrews 12:6-12. Remember, the purpose of conviction is repentance and restoration. If you have repented, let Him restore you. Let Him heal you. He doesn't want you to remain stuck. He wants you to be changed so that you can bear fruit, comfort others, and continue the work of ministry.

Think about the times you have fallen. Has God convicted you? Did you hear His voice and feel His hand showing you your disobedience, drawing you back to Him? Did that conviction result in repentance, or are you still clinging to the choices you made, either too ashamed to face them or holding onto them as a coping mechanism you cannot quite release? If you repented, have you allowed Him to heal and restore, or are you continuing to punish yourself, believing God cannot redeem you? He can. He longs to restore fellowship with you, His child.

Discipline isn't always fun. But if we can embrace it, and Him, instead of running or being filled with resentment, we are freed. His forgiveness empowers us to move forward. He has a plan for every person who belongs to Him. That plan will always include fulfilling His Great Commission. After the discipline comes peace, and then we are ready to show Him to others.

Words from the Living Water

1. Think about a time in your life when you made sinful choices. Did God convict? How did you hear His voice? What was your response?

2. It seems strange, the idea that discipline is a *good* thing. But we see in Hebrews 12:6-12. Read this passage and list the benefits of being God's child and receiving His discipline.

3. Psalm 119:11 says, "I have treasured Your word in my heart, so that I may not sin against You." (NASB). Choose a verse from this chapter to memorize and meditate on this week.

Nave/What Happens After the Well

Chapter 3: The Fruit of Repentance

"Therefore produce fruit consistent with repentance." Matthew 3:8, NASB

The dictionary defines repentance as sincere regret or remorse. Wikipedia defines it below:
"The activity of reviewing one's actions and feeling contrition or regret for past wrongs, which is accompanied by a commitment to and actual actions that show and prove a change for the better."[1]

Repentance is a necessary response to sin. Over and over the Bible tells us about the necessity of true repentance, from the repeated stories of Israel's repentance each time they forgot God, to Jesus' parables, including the parable of the Pharisee and the tax collector. We are commanded to repent. Then, like John the Baptist said in Matthew 3, we are to bear fruit in keeping with repentance. Bearing the fruit of that repentance moves us forward, and we'll be talking more about that in this chapter.

But first, let's talk about what real repentance is. Here is an excellent quote by Albert Martin:

---

[1] *Repentance: https://en.wikipedia.org/wiki/Repentance*

"Repentance is being sorry enough to quit your sin. You will never know the forgiving mercy of God while you are still wedded to your sins. Repentance is the soul's divorce from sin, but it will always be joined to faith. Repentance that is not joined to faith is a legalistic repentance. Professed faith that is not joined to repentance is a spurious faith, for true faith is faith in Christ to save me not in but from my sin. Repentance and faith are inseparable, and "unless you repent you will all likewise perish" (Luke 13:3)."[2]

There's a lot in that quote - a lot of really good theology. And it echoes that Wikipedia definition which, unexpectedly, is in line with scripture. True repentance goes beyond just a feeling. It's a turning, a quitting, a commitment, and action. And according to Martin, it is inextricably linked to faith.

I want to get literal and practical because I think a real understanding of repentance is vital to leaving sin behind. When I say leaving sin behind, I don't just mean stopping. I mean leaving behind the weight that keeps us stuck feeling the shame of condemnation. Remember, as Romans 8:1 says, "There is therefore now no condemnation for those who are in Christ Jesus." It also means leaving behind the thinking and environment that led us to sin in the first place.

I read two Psalms over and over when I was broken over my own sin - Psalm 32 and Psalm 51. They both provide not only comfort but a blueprint of real repentance and what it entails. I encourage you to take a moment, grab your Bible or your phone and Google, and read both of these Psalms.

Let's look at Psalm 32. Verses three and four paint a vivid picture of the conviction we discussed in chapter two. David elaborates on how conviction brought him to a crisis point.

"When I kept silent about my sin, my body wasted away
Through my groaning all day long.
For day and night Your hand was heavy upon me;
My vitality failed as with the dry heat of summer."
VV 2-3

---

[2] *Albert Martin* https://www.azquotes.com/author/54912-Albert_Martin

Verse five gives us the first step of repentance - acknowledging our sin:

"I acknowledged my sin to You,
And I did not hide my guilt;
I said, "I will confess my wrongdoings to the Lord;"
And You forgave the guilt of my sin."

Sin needs to be exposed to the light. Like mold, it thrives in darkness. Until we are willing to take that sin out of hiding and call it what it is, we cannot reach that place of repentance. Once we have exposed it to honesty, we need to confess our sin to God. I John 1:9 tells us that if we confess our sins, God is faithful and just to forgive us and cleanse us from all unrighteousness. *If* we confess. And that means we agree with God's assessment of our sin.

Verse 6 of Psalm 32 gives us an interesting warning:

"Therefore, let everyone who is godly pray to You in a time when You may be found;
Certainly, in a flood of great waters, they will not reach him."

This suggests that God doesn't wait forever. His conviction and pursuit are not indefinite. Isaiah echoes this sentiment in chapter 43, verses 6-7 when it says, "Seek the Lord while He may be found; Call upon Him while He is near." (NASB). When God pricks your heart, respond.

Psalm 51 may be more familiar to many of us. This is said to be the Psalm that David wrote after Nathan confronted him about his affair with Bathsheba and his murder of Uriah. David, God's anointed king of Israel, had decided to stay in the palace instead of doing what kings normally did during a war: go to the battlefield with their men. One night he saw Bathsheba bathing on her roof. He liked what he saw, so he sent for her. The problem? Both of them were married to someone else. In fact, Bathsheba's husband, Uriah, was on the battlefield fighting for David. David slept with Bathsheba, and she became pregnant.

Instead of owning up to his sin, David had Uriah brought home for some rest. He hoped that Bathsheba and Uriah would be intimate, and then they could claim that the baby was Uriah's. However, Uriah was a diligent soldier. He refused to enjoy his wife while his brothers were risking their lives on the battlefield. So David sent word to have Uriah put on the front lines of the battle where he would almost certainly be killed. His plan worked. Uriah was killed in battle, and David brought his widow to the palace for "comfort." He did all of this scheming to cover up his sin.

Hebrews 12 tells us God always chastens his children. In II Samuel 12, Nathan confronts David about his sin with a very poignant story about a family and their beloved lamb. Despite all of David's attempts to hide his sin, God brought it into the light. Psalm 51 is David's response of repentance.

> "Be gracious to me, God, according to Your faithfulness;
> According to the greatness of Your compassion, wipe out my wrongdoings.
> Wash me thoroughly from my guilt
> And cleanse me from my sin."
> Psalm 51:1-2

In the first two verses, David begs God for forgiveness and mercy. He appeals to God's faithfulness and asks God to cleanse him of his sin. He acknowledges his guilt.

> "For I know my wrongdoings,
> And my sin is constantly before me."
> V 3

David couldn't escape his sin. His Father was convicting him, reminding him. Just like I couldn't outrun God's conviction in that parking lot, David couldn't outrun God either.

> "Against You, You only, I have sinned
> And done what is evil in Your sight,

So that You are justified when You speak
And blameless when You judge."
V 4

Verse 4 is important. There are two essential points to see here. First, David understood who, ultimately, he had sinned against. His statement does not mean that the pain he inflicted on others is insignificant. David's sin gravely hurt Bathsheba, Uriah, and the nation as a whole. But at the core, he had rebelled against God. Until he acknowledged that truth, he couldn't even begin to address all the other pain he caused. Like David, when we sin, whether it's adultery, stealing, gossip, or pride, we are ultimately sinning against the One who created us.

The second part of the verse is important because of the humility and thinking we adopt when we are truly repentant. He says to God - You are justified in whatever you do with me and however you judge me. He didn't try to negotiate or mitigate his actions. He didn't say, "That's not fair!" when the consequences came. And they came harshly. The baby that he and Bathsheba created died just days after birth. And later, another child from their union betrayed David and attempted to overthrow him, creating upheaval in Israel. Then of course there was the upheaval in David's household and the painful rebuke from Nathan.

Sin has consequences. Yes, Jesus's work on the cross saves us from the eternal consequences of sin. But we are not exempt from the earthly consequences of our choices. Even if a bank robber is sincerely sorry for his crime, he will still serve his sentence. Marriages may still end, finances may still be devastated, and relationships may still be broken.

But David doesn't stay in the mire of the consequences. That's where the fruit of his repentance begins to show. Look at what he says in the verses that follow. In verse six, he acknowledges the importance of honesty, and he realizes he needs God's wisdom. In verse seven, he declares that only God can cleanse and purify him from his sin.

And of all the verses in Psalm 51, I think verse 8 may be my favorite:

"Let me hear joy and gladness,
Let the bones You have broken rejoice."

That last part is such a beautiful redemptive picture - let the bones You have broken rejoice. God breaks us and brings us to repentance, and then He puts those pieces back together. We rejoice in the brokenness because it leads us to repentance and back into fellowship with Him. The same Father who causes us to mourn over our sin will revive us and cause us to be joyful again.

David's heart is evident in the requests he makes toward the end of this Psalm:

- Hide Your face from my sins
- Wipe out all my guilty deeds
- Create in me a clean heart
- Renew a right spirit in me
- Don't cast me away from Your presence
- Don't take your spirit from me
- Restore the joy of my salvation
- Give me a willing spirit

David wants God to change him. Not his circumstances - him. He wants God to be near to Him, to make Him clean, to make Him faithful again. He wants to right his relationship with his Father. Then he transitions into asking God for a willing spirit. But a willing spirit to do what?

- I will teach wrongdoers Your ways
- My tongue will joyfully sing of Your righteousness
- Open my lips so my mouth may declare Your praise

Does this sound like someone who was hiding in the background because he had gone too far for God to do anything with him? No. David was still king, appointed by God. He still had work to do, and he was still a man after God's own heart. God continued to use him. He, in His mercy, even allowed David to have another son - Solomon - who God also used mightily, even though he too was imperfect.

When I feel the weight of my choices, one of the first questions I ask is, "Have I truly repented? Have I acknowledged and confessed my sin? Have I turned away from it, or am I still holding on to the control or security I thought it afforded me?" Or maybe I'm so busy trying to make sure it stays hidden, I am not bearing the fruit of repentance. Psalm 66:18 cuts to the core of this: "If I regard (see: hide, cherish, protect, keep as a failsafe, justify, defend) wickedness in my heart, the Lord will not hear."

Before we leave the fruits of repentance, we need to talk about amends. Making amends is a tricky subject, but it is important to address it, particularly when our choices have affected others. Sometimes amends are obvious and tangible. Other times they aren't as apparent. So we'll look at two people in the Bible who needed to make amends.

We'll begin with Zacchaeus. You can find his story in Luke 19:1-10, but I'll summarize it a bit.

Zacchaeus was a tax collector. Actually, he wasn't just a tax collector - he was the chief tax collector. He was also very wealthy. How did he become so wealthy, you ask? He told people they owed more taxes than they actually did, and he pocketed the difference between what they owed and what he collected. He stole from the citizens. Sadly, at the time, this was a pretty common tactic among tax collectors. As a result, people generally hated them. Their dishonesty and fraudulent behaviors were public knowledge. However, the people also feared tax collectors, so they didn't dare confront them with their deception. Much like we are with the IRS at times, they were afraid of the power the tax collectors could wield - the power to make their lives miserable.

Zacchaeus heard Jesus was coming to town, so he climbed a tree to get a better view. He was short, but I also have to wonder if he also thought the tree might be a good hiding place from which to watch. If you read Luke 18, you'll see that Jesus had been preaching some pretty heavy stuff: persistence in prayer, humility, choosing riches over God's kingdom. That last one probably stepped on Zacchaeus's toes a bit.

Then Jesus goes right up to the tree and calls to Zacchaeus, "Hey, Zacchaeus! Climb down from there. I'm coming to your house!"

Of course, Zacchaeus scrambles down, and they make their way to his home. Zacchaeus was excited. However, look at what verse 7 says. "When the people saw this, they began to complain, saying, 'He has gone in to be the guest of a sinner!'"

What does Zacchaeus say after his encounter with Jesus? He says, "Behold, Lord, half of my possessions I am giving to the poor, and if I have extorted anything from anyone, I am giving back four times as much."

Jesus's response was to declare that salvation had come to Zacchaeus's house and to reiterate that He had come to earth to seek and to save.

I want to be clear: salvation didn't come to Zacchaeus because he repaid the money. He repaid what he had stolen *because* he had experienced salvation. His actions were the outward evidence of his inward transformation. He was bearing fruit in keeping with repentance. Zacchaeus had a tangible way to make amends. He could repay over and above what he had taken from others. He even gave a large portion of all his wealth to the poor. This was further evidence of how Jesus had completely transformed Zacchaeus' priorities.

Sometimes our choices need tangible amends. If we stole an item, we need to return it. If we spread a false rumor, we need to set the record straight. Even if the information was true, gossip is also a sin, and we need to apologize. If we left the scene of a fender bender, we need to take the necessary legal steps. If we hurt someone, we need to acknowledge it, taking full responsibility for our actions. These are practical and necessary ways to bear the fruit of repentance. But sometimes it isn't so clear-cut. Sometimes there is no item to return or no repair to pay for. What do we do then?

The story of Saul, who later became Paul, can give us some guidance. The first time we see him, he is holding the cloaks of others while they stone the apostle Stephen to death. He stood there, in full approval of this stoning, as Stephen had been preaching the gospel about this Jesus, who was still a threat to the Jews even after they crucified Him. But, as we see in Acts 8, it goes farther than that:

"But Saul began ravaging the church, entering house after house; and he would drag away men and women and put them in prison." Acts 8:3

Saul actively and aggressively persecuted the early church and early believers. He approved when Christians were imprisoned and killed, and he actively looked for believers from whom he could exact punishment.

Then, in Acts 9, Saul encounters Jesus on the road to Damascus, and he is struck blind. He sees the truth of what he has done and hears Jesus's voice. And like anyone whose life has been changed, he wants to share his transformation and serve the Savior. But how could he? How could Paul ever make amends? He couldn't bring back Stephen. Even if he had the power to release all the Christians from prison, he couldn't undo their trauma. He couldn't turn back time. The early believers were afraid of him. What could he do?

He waited. When we see Paul after his Damascus road experience, he is staying at the home of a man named Judas. We don't know much about Judas except that he allowed Paul to stay with him. Paul was still blind. He wasn't preaching yet. He was waiting for God's direction. And that direction came in the form of a vision that promised a visitor named Ananias.

God spoke to Ananias and told him to go "inquire at the house of Judas for a man from Tarsus named Saul, for he is praying." Paul wasn't twiddling his thumbs in the dark, we see. He was praying. Paul also listened and learned. Ananias came and healed Paul's blindness, and he had important words for Paul:

"So Ananias departed and entered the house, and after laying his hands on him said, 'Brother Saul, the Lord Jesus, who appeared to you on the road by which you were coming, has sent me so that you may regain your sight and be filled with the Holy Spirit.'" Acts 9:17

The passage goes on to say that Paul spent several days with the disciples who were in Damascus. Who knows how many times he had to retell his story or how many questions they asked him. I would imagine Ananias had to repeat his story a few times too, since he brought to them the great persecutor of the church. Even after Paul began preaching the gospel, it took time for some of those early believers to trust him. Finally, Barnabas, a respected apostle, spoke on his behalf.

Paul couldn't undo his prior actions. So his *life* had to be the amends. His service, his commitment to the gospel, his letters to the churches, and his sacrifice were the actions that healed the hurts. And in the end, the early believers supported him, even helping him to escape from those who were plotting Paul's death.

Amends are an important part of bearing the fruit of repentance. Not just for the sake of our fellowship with God, but also the sake of our fellowship with others. If you have confessed and turned from your sin and your past choices, but something is still missing, still keeping you from moving forward, ask yourself if you need to make amends. Do you need to repay something or make something right? Do you need to wait and pray for God's direction? Maybe you need to find a wise, godly mentor to help you work through restoration and reconciliation.

How can you begin and continue to bear the fruit of repentance? How can you bring tangibility to your confession of and turning from sin? Are there practical amends you can make? How can you immerse yourself in the Living Water?

Words from Living Water

1. Reread Matthew 3:8. What are some tangible fruits that we can produce in keeping with repentance in our own lives and toward others?

2. David was so transparent in his grief over his sin. What are some of the lessons he learned about his sin and how it affected his life as written in Psalm 32?

3. What distinguishes true repentance from just feeling bad, feeling guilty, or being sorry? What Scripture did we see in chapter three that helps to answer this question?

Nave/What Happens After the Well

CH 4: Women of Redemption

The Bible is full of people who have fallen, experienced pain, or have been far from God who He has brought near again. I want to focus on three women who God used after redeeming them from differing circumstances and restoring to them a victorious life. One was a prostitute, one was a grieving widow, and one was healed of seven demons. Let's look into the lives of Rahab, Naomi, and Mary Magdalene.

Rahab the prostitute

In the book of Joshua, we see a people who have wandered in the desert for 40 years. They wandered because they didn't believe God. It's kind of crazy to think that a people who saw the plagues, were rescued from Egypt, crossed the Red Sea on dry land, were guided by clouds and fire, and had manna sent from Heaven, fumbled their faith on the five-yard line. God had done amazing, miraculous things in their sight, but when that first group of spies saw Jericho, they cried, "They're giants! We're doomed!" And so they wandered.

It seems crazy until I think about all the ways God has cared for me, and yet when crises come or when God doesn't respond in the way and time I thought He would, I am not always so different from that first group of spies. And then I end up wandering as well.

At any rate, the Israelites have come back to the edge of Jericho, and this time Joshua sent only two spies to go to the city. Two spies in a strange place where their lives would be in danger. How in the world would God keep them safe within the walls and then deliver them back to Joshua?

The first verse of Joshua chapter 2 tells us, *They went to the home of Rahab, the prostitute.* Some scholars parse the word for prostitute here. They speculate whether she was simply a prostitute or if she was associated with one of the pagan sects that included prostitution in their rituals. Some hypothesized that she was simply an innkeeper where there happened to be a brothel. Whatever the particulars, Rahab was a pagan woman who was well-known for - at the very least - running an immoral business.

How do we know she was well-known? Well, the next few verses tell us that the leaders of the city, sent by the king, came to her door to ask her about the two spies. She was prominent, and word of anything happening at her door obviously traveled quickly. It's not surprising that the king's men would ask about the strangers.

What is surprising *is* her response. She says, "They were here, but they went that way. If you hurry, you can catch them!" She sent them in the wrong direction, and then she went and alerted the two spies, who were hiding on her roof underneath some thatch covering. Why would she endanger herself by lying to the king's men and protecting two strangers?

Take a look at verses 9-11 of chapter 2:

"And (Rahab) said to the men, 'I know that the Lord has given you the land, and that the terror of you has fallen on us, and that all the inhabitants of the land have despaired because of you. For we have heard how the Lord dried up the water of the Red Sea before you when you came out of Egypt, and what you did to the two kings of the Amorites who were beyond the Jordan, to Sihon and Og, whom you utterly destroyed. When we heard these reports, our hearts melted and no courage remained in anyone any longer because of you; for the Lord your God, He is God in heaven above and on earth below.'" Joshua 2:9-11

Rahab believed. She heard of the works of the Israelites' God, and she knew in her heart that Jehovah God was the Lord of Heaven and earth. And so she hid the spies and helped them to escape. But she didn't stop there. Now, Rahab could have been so embarrassed by her occupation that she didn't bother asking for anything. I mean, she was a prostitute! Surely she had no business asking God's agents for anything.

She did ask, however. And not just for herself. She asked the spies to promise to save her and her family from Jericho when the walls fell. She wanted all of them to be spared. This is what happens when someone realizes that God can rescue them - they want the people they love to share in that gift.

The men made her a promise. They told her to tie a scarlet rope to her window, and they promised that every member of her family who was in her house where the rope was tied would be spared and taken safely out of Jericho.

This may seem like a no-brainer, but really think about it. Her family lived in the most fortified, protected, unbreachable city in the region. The wall around Jericho was so thick, Rahab's house sat on it. So how do you think she convinced her family that a big group of vagabonds (who ran away 40 years before) was going to breach the city simply by marching around it? These Israelites were going to conquer the safest city in the land? But Rahab convinced them to have faith. There's no way they would have believed her story unless they believed the God of the Israelites was big enough to knock down the walls. Her faith changed their lives. Take a look at chapter 6:

"And Joshua said to the two men who had spied out the land, 'Go into the prostitute's house and bring the woman and all she has out of there, just as you have sworn to her.' So the young men who were spies went in and brought out Rahab, her father, her mother, her brothers, and all she had; they also brought out all her relatives and placed them outside the camp of Israel. Then they burned the city with fire, and all that was in it. Only the silver and gold, and the articles of bronze and iron, they put into the treasury of the house of the Lord. However, Rahab the prostitute and her father's household and all she had, Joshua spared; and she has lived in the midst of Israel to this day, because she hid the messengers whom Joshua sent to spy out Jericho." VV 22-25

Her father. Mother, brothers, and other members of her family, had escaped Jericho with the Israelites. And they weren't just rescued and dropped off at the nearest bus station. Rahab spent the rest of her days with the Israelites. She married an Israelite. Now, turn to Matthew chapter 1. Look at the verses:

"Salmon fathered Boaz by Rahab, Boaz fathered Obed by Ruth, and Obed fathered Jesse. Jesse fathered David the king." VV 5-6

David became king of Israel. And not only that, but it was also through David's lineage that the Savior came - Jesus. Rahab, the former prostitute, was one of only two women who are named in the lineage of Christ in Matthew chapter 1. No shrinking on the shelf due to her past for Rahab. Her descendants gave birth to the Messiah!

Naomi, bitter from loss
The Book of Ruth is a wonderful story of restoration and love. In it, Ruth, a Moabite woman, returns to Judah with her mother-in-law after the death of her husband. She works in the fields to help provide for herself and Naomi. Boaz, a relative of Naomi's, notices Ruth's diligence and protects her. Naomi understands what this protection means.

She advises Ruth to go to the threshing floor and lay at Boaz's feet while he sleeps. Now *that's* an unusual way of letting a man know you're interested! Boaz knows there is one man who is a closer relative to Naomi than he is, so he goes to the city gate and arranges to take this relative's place in marrying Ruth. He is often referred to as Ruth's "kinsman-redeemer." At the end of the story, we see that Boaz and Ruth had a son named Obed. Obed had a son named Jesse. Jesse was the father of King David.

However, it isn't Ruth's story I want to talk about in this section; it's Naomi's. Let's start a little before the beginning.

There was a famine in Judah. Naomi, her husband Elimelech, and their two sons were in peril along with the rest of the Israelites. However, while the other Israelites stayed to wait through the famine together, Elimelech was impatient. He heard that things were much more prosperous in the land of Moab, a pagan city. He moved his family away from everything and everyone they knew and settled them in Moab. Sadly, a year or so later, Elimelech died, leaving Naomi a widow with two sons and a crop already planted. They couldn't go back to Judah with crops in the ground, so they stayed.

Now, during this time, God was very particular about His people. He knew them. As we can see throughout the Old Testament, they were very susceptible to their environment. If they blended their lives with those who worshiped false gods, they always seemed to get swept up into the false worship too. So God forbade His people from intermarrying. It wasn't a racial issue, it was a spiritual one. If a person converted to Judaism beforehand, the marriage was fine. But God's people were not to marry pagans. In a way, it was much like God's New Testament command for Christians not to be unequally yoked in marriage to non-Christians. This is why it is wise for a Christian to only date another believer.

Naomi was in Moab, and her sons were of age. Like any man, they wanted to marry a woman and have a family. There were no Israelite women nearby, so they did what God knew they would do. They married Moabite women. Naomi must have been upset by this. Or maybe she wasn't. Maybe she had grown used to the ways of the people around her as well. The women her sons married were kind, and Naomi grew to love them as daughters.

Then tragedy struck again. First, Ruth's husband died, and then Orpah's husband died. They were three women with no husbands to protect them or provide for them. It wasn't 2021. They needed that provision and protection. Naomi finally realized she needed to go back to her own family in Judah. She told both Ruth and Orpah to go back to their Moabite families. She said, "I'm too old to have more sons for you to marry!" Both of them longed to stay with her, but Orpah finally relented and left. Ruth, however, was determined to stay with Naomi. She said to the woman, "Wherever you go, I will go. Wherever you stay, I will stay. Your people are my people, and your God is my God." This beautiful sentiment has become a song sung at many weddings, including my own parents' wedding almost 60 years ago.

This is usually where the story becomes about Ruth. But let's stay with Naomi. Naomi and Ruth returned to Judah. When they arrived, Naomi's friends and family exclaimed, "Can this be Naomi? She has returned!" Many were glad to see her and rejoiced. I am sure some also clucked their tongues and shook their heads, thinking of "I told you so" and looking askance at the Moabite woman who was with her. Naomi's response to all of them was bitter:

"But she said to them, 'Do not call me Naomi; call me Mara, for the Almighty has dealt very bitterly with me. I went away full, but the Lord has brought me back empty. Why do you call me Naomi, since the Lord has testified against me and the Almighty has afflicted me?'"
Ruth 1:20-21

I'll confess when I was younger - a lot younger - I was a bit judgmental about Naomi's response. After all, she was the one who moved to a pagan land. She let her sons mingle with and marry the Moabite women. Besides, tragedies happen. Surely it wasn't appropriate for her to blame God?

Now that I've lived more than half a century outside the comfortable bubble of my close-knit family circle, and I've experienced several crises, tragedies, unchangeable circumstances, and failures, I understand Naomi's state of mind much better. Naomi wasn't just reacting out of bitterness. There was also grief, regret, a lack of control over her life, and shame.

Mara - the name meant "bitter" in the Hebrew language of the time. And honestly, I can understand Naomi's sentiment. I have had times in my own life when the pain and grief, the life I never thought I'd live, and my own choices seemed so foreign, I felt like a different person. In fact, for several years, it was painful to look back at the Laurie of her twenties in light of what I had become. How could they both be me? That previous, faithful, "blameless" Laurie had died it seemed. Of course, the truth is that 25-year-old

Laurie wasn't blameless either. Romans 3 makes that abundantly and universally clear.

For Naomi, coming back home as a different woman had to be difficult. Had it not been for Ruth, things could have been even worse. Even with her widowed daughter-in-law, it must have felt as if a life of joy was over for Naomi.

But as they settled into their new life in Judah, as Ruth worked, and as Naomi healed, things began to change. I wish we knew more about the day-to-day of Naomi's life during this transition. Did her friends and family visit her to encourage her and remind her of God's faithfulness? She was back in her home, with time to grieve and examine her life, and gradually she changed. The inward bitterness gave way to a more outward focus. And when Ruth needed her wisdom, Naomi was ready to give it.

After Boaz met with the closest relative and married Ruth, Naomi knew her life was going to be more hopeful. Then, when Ruth bore a son, we can see her joy:

"Then the women said to Naomi, 'Blessed is the Lord who has not left you without a redeemer today and may his name become famous in Israel. May he also be to you one who restores life and sustains your old age; for your daughter-in-law, who loves you and is better to you than seven sons, has given birth to him.' Then Naomi took the child and laid him in her lap, and became his nurse." Ruth 4:14-16

So Naomi, a woman who returned to Judah broken, is now blessed with a loyal daughter-in-law in Ruth and her husband Boaz, who treats Naomi as a mother, and a grandson who was the grandfather of David, from whose line Jesus was born.

Mary Magdalene, the woman with seven demons

One of the hardest aspects of falling and its fallout - from a human perspective - is the crushing of pride and the humiliation we may experience. We tend to cover our sins because of pride and in order to avoid humiliation. We all care more than we would like to admit about how others view us. Even those who loudly proclaim, "I don't care what anyone thinks!" often do so because they are resisting the pain of others' rejection or judgment. It's one of the reasons we so vehemently misuse that verse in Matthew 7: "Judge not." None of us like to be the object of scrutiny, judgment, or humiliation.

So imagine what it must have been like to be Mary Magdalene. Many Bible scholars believe that she may have been wealthy or prominent due to the name or term "Magdalene." People knew who she was. However, her wealth and possible prominence weren't what initially defined her in the Bible. Mary Magdalene was demon-possessed. And she wasn't just possessed by one demon - she was possessed by seven demons. Luke 8 tells us:

"Soon afterward, Jesus began going around from one city and village to another, proclaiming and preaching the kingdom of God. The twelve were with Him, and also some women who had been healed of evil spirits and sicknesses: Mary who was called Magdalene, from whom seven demons had gone out, and Joanna the wife of Chuza, Herod's steward, and Susanna, and many others who were contributing to their support out of their private means." VV 1-3

Mary Magdalene was likely in intense, painful, and very public torment. I'm sure the people in the community gave her a wide berth and warned their children to stay away from her. The Bible gives us another example of someone possessed by multiple demons, and he ran naked through graveyards, cutting himself with stones! Demon-possession was not a pretty picture.

Then Jesus healed her and cast out all seven demons. She was once again in her right mind, and she became a believer. She followed Jesus for the rest of His life on earth. In addition, she helped support His ministry out of her private means, giving more credence to her likely being wealthy. Mary Magdalene was with Jesus' mother when He died, and she was the first to see Jesus after His resurrection from the dead.

Let's step back just a bit. Think about this. She began following Jesus as soon as she was healed and freed of the demons. And Jesus welcomed her. This may not seem like a big deal in

2021, but that was a different time with different societal norms. First, Mary was a woman. Women were not seen as important or significant in many respects. Of course, Jesus defied this social convention on more than one occasion, including His encounter with the woman at the well. He also publicly defended the woman caught in adultery. He allowed a fallen woman, thankful for redemption, to pour expensive oil on His feet, an act the Pharisees criticized.

Mary Magdalene had been a very public spectacle as a demon-possessed woman. She had a reputation. Did Jesus really want to connect Himself and His reputation with someone so recently deranged? What would people think, seeing Him with that woman everyone thought was "crazy?" Jesus wasn't concerned about those things. He didn't tell her to lie low and come see Him once the gossip had died down. He had healed and transformed her. She was a believer. She had gifts that would benefit His ministry and impact others. He welcomed her.

Come to think of it, with our modern technology, cancel culture, and the long memory humans tend to have, I'm not sure that it would have been easy for Mary to immediately follow Jesus in 2021 either. Redemption - public redemption, is almost impossible in our modern contradiction of no moral absolutes versus "one wrong move, and you're viral."

In Mary's case, once again we have someone whom no one would have described as "ministry material" who plays a significant role in God's plan. Like Rahab, who rescued the spies, Mary was integral, being the first to see Jesus after His resurrection. These women were God's instruments. This should give us joy. As we look at what God has redeemed us *from*, the stories of Rahab, Naomi, and Mary Magdalene should propel us toward what Christ redeemed us *for* - for His glory and work in His kingdom.

All of these women: Rahab, Naomi, and Mary Magdalene faced painful, sinful, scandalous pasts. And each of them was lovingly rescued and restored by God. What's more, each of them was connected to Jesus, as part of the lineage from which He was born and as the first to see Him after he rose from the dead.

Words from Living Water

1. What do Rahab and Ruth have in common? What is the significance of this commonality?

2. Think about Naomi's heart as she returned to her home. Have you ever felt as she did, bitter and broken down from life? How can God's Word comfort us in times like this? How does the story of Naomi, Ruth, and Boaz give you hope?

3. In your own quiet times in God's Word, have you encountered other women who were imperfect but mightily used by God? Who are they? Where can we find their stories? Are there any women in your own life who you know have struggled but who God uses to minister to others?

Chapter 5: Believers Who Blew It

You may have noticed, I enjoy alliteration. I blame the many preachers I have heard over the years who love to alliterate their sermon points. Plus, it's fun!

If I had to pick a portion of this book that has been closest to my own heart and my biggest personal struggle, it would probably be this chapter. I think there is a whole silent subset of Christians who struggle with this.

See, for me, it's easy to understand how God uses someone who was this horrible, sinful nonbeliever and then comes to Christ and is transformed. They have such wonderful stories to tell. And those awful choices they made? Lost people are expected to be sinful, right?

But what about the Christian who walks through a season of dark disobedience? What about the Sunday School teacher who ended up battling addiction? The choir member who had an affair? The deacon whose financial crisis led him to steal or defraud? The church member with the anger problem?

We celebrate the drug addict who is dramatically saved and kicks the habit. Not so much the former Bible study leader who torpedoed their personal life through three or four years of rebellion. In fact, some churches simply say, "they were never saved to begin with," as if saved people cannot possibly be trapped in sin. A practicing Christian would "know better." And even if they come back to Christ, surely they are now disqualified. They gave Jesus a bad name. Who could ever trust them and who they are now?

And for those of us who had that dark period full of choices we deeply regret, we ask the same questions about ourselves. How could we? What was *wrong* with us? We've sullied the name of Christ. Can we ever trust ourselves? Who do we think we are, talking about the Bible or sin or Jesus after what we did? We should get out of the way so the real Christians can do the work. Besides, our brothers and sisters in Christ - not to mention the rest of the world - don't want to hear from us, of all people.

Many years ago, I used to teach, disciple, write Bible studies, and serve. Then I went through my own period of rebellion. I repented, but I was quiet. Much like Paul, I needed to pray and wait. Then, a couple of years ago, I began having the desire to teach. I squelched it, didn't say anything, and just continued to stay in the background. Yes, I had taught. But that was *before* I blew it. That was the good Laurie, the clean Laurie. I didn't mention the desire to anyone because I felt unworthy. Not that I would have before either. It has never been my personality to *ask* to teach, to sing a solo, to be out front. But especially not now.

Except that the pastor came to me and asked me to pray about teaching a women's Sunday School class. So I prayed. After I asked the pastor if he was sure he wanted "someone like me" to teach the Bible? He knew enough about my period of rebellion to know I was not a pristine bastion of uninterrupted faithfulness. When he said, yes, he was sure, I asked my mother. She said yes too. My wise mother said to stop focusing on the past. I asked a couple of honest friends who I knew wouldn't be afraid to hurt my feelings (smile). They said yes. I should stop fixating on the sin that Christ had covered.

This was a real struggle for me. I knew in my head that the condemning voices weren't God's voice, that they were lying to me. And to be honest, that voice is too often echoed in the Christian community. *Did they nominate him to be a deacon? Don't they know about...She's singing a solo? Why, she used to sing in bars!!* We are not kind to the fallen, even after they repent. Not to mention how many people may have had front row seats - whether in person or digitally - to my failings. If I stepped out presumptuously and tried to minister, would I awake the sleeping giants of condemnation?

Yes, we should take sin seriously. We should not "trample afresh the blood of Christ" (Hebrews 10:29). We should fully repent and turn from sin, taking full responsibility for our actions. We should accept the consequences and seek to make amends. That crucial step is important. We need to be willing to take *time* for restoration.

Try as I might, I could find no biblical support for my fear or the idea that one too many sins mean you lose your worker card and go to the back of the room. I couldn't find a single example of Jesus saying, "Not you! You're a liability. You need to stop talking about me. I can't use you after all you did."

So, let's take a look at some biblical examples of believers who blew it and still did great things for the kingdom of God.

Peter, the disciple with the big mouth

Ah, Peter. He preached at Pentecost when the flaming tongues came down and thousands were saved. He did miracles. He was one of the three disciples closest to Jesus. He died a martyr for his faith. But, oh dear, that mouth, as the adage (and meme) says. He spoke before he thought, acted before he thought, and wielded a sword before he thought.

Of all the cringe-worthy things Peter did, however, the most heartbreaking was his denial of Jesus.

The night before Jesus's crucifixion, the disciples met in an upper room for fellowship. It was particularly poignant because Jesus knew it would be the last time they were together before His crucifixion. This was the last time He would dine with them, teach them, or pray with them before He was arrested. Jesus broke the bread and shared the wine as symbols of what was about to happen.

During this final supper, Jesus made a shocking declaration: One of you will betray me this night. Of course, everyone wanted to know who it was. "Is it me, Lord?" Then, as he tended to do, Peter spoke up. "I'd never betray you, Lord!" As we say in the south, bless his heart. Jesus responded, as He always does, with the truth:

"And Jesus said to him, 'Truly I say to you, that this very night before a rooster crows twice, you yourself will deny Me three times.'" Mark 14:30, NASB

Now, the promised Messiah, the Son of God, has just told Peter what was going to happen. So Peter bowed his head humbly and told Jesus he was sorry, right?
Umm...no. He argued with Jesus:

"But Peter repeatedly said insistently, 'Even if I have to die with You, I will not deny You!' And they all were saying the same thing as well." Mark 14:31, NASB

That verse strikes me because I identify with poor Peter. I grew up in church, studied my Bible, went on mission trips, loved Jesus, and followed Him for many years. Sure, I might occasionally slip and gossip or lose my temper while driving behind a slowpoke. But there was no way I'd be blind enough to really blow it. I had boundaries. I knew better. I didn't have to worry about *real* sin.
Peter thought so too. He left the garden that night upset but still convinced he was Jesus' most faithful follower. He had tried to defend Jesus with a sword while everyone else just stood there. Sure, he was afraid of what would happen. But he would just lie low, stay close to the goings-on, and see what happened to Jesus.
So he must have been caught off guard when that first person recognized him. "Hey, I've seen you! You're one of those people who follow Jesus around!"
"No, not me," Peter replied. "I don't know that guy."
Now, a smart person would have faded away somewhere after being recognized once. But not Peter. He stayed, and he even gathered with others around a fire. In addition, since they had just discussed Peter's denial, he should have been grief-stricken over the betrayal and purposed not to let it happen again. But he wasn't.

He denied Jesus two more times, growing angrier and crasser each time.

Then the rooster crowed. And Peter was snapped out of his panic. He realized what he had done and grieved terribly.

I have to wonder if Peter had believed Jesus's warning and understood that he was fallible and vulnerable, would things have been different? Would he have found another place to hide instead of hanging around where he would be recognized? Would he have prepared an answer for possible questions?

Instead, he was sure he was immune to such a grievous error. He became a textbook example of the verse, *"Pride goes before destruction, and a haughty spirit before stumbling." Proverbs 16:18, NASB*

As I look back on some of my choices, I see so many tiny steps, so many warnings and red flags leading up to my actual crushing decisions. I ignored them because I thought I could handle it. I'd never do *that*. Pride makes us so blind. So does complacency. So does fear.

I think that's why Peter reacted the way he did. He was terrified, and that fear made him vulnerable. He had spent three years following the Messiah, and now his Messiah had been arrested and was being tried before both Roman and religious courts. There was talk of crucifixion. If they planned to kill Jesus, what would they do to his followers?

Peter was vulnerable, and he wasn't prepared. Satan loves that perfect storm combination. It's when he whispers to us that we deserve "that," that, of course, it's okay to protect ourselves, and no one will know. I can even picture Peter internally justifying his actions. "I can't help Jesus if I'm dead or in prison. I have to be careful."

As I child I learned the almost universally known children's song, "Jesus Loves Me." You may have learned it as well. There's a line that applies to the place Peter found himself - the place we sometimes find ourselves. "In our weakness He is strong."

It's a simple line from a children's song, but it is still true. He knows when we are weak, vulnerable, tired, and frustrated. And that's when He wants to step in and be our strength. I Corinthians 10:13 gives us a wonderful promise:

"No temptation has overtaken you except something common to mankind; and God is faithful, so He will not allow you to be tempted beyond what you are able, but with the temptation will provide the way of escape also, so that you will be able to endure it." NASB

I don't want to go too far off the main topic here, but I think this verse has some vital truths for us to absorb and cling to when we are weak. Especially after we've failed, one of two things can happen. We can focus on what "made" us vulnerable, how God didn't fix it, how someone let us down, and so we had to figure it out ourselves. I've walked that road, and it doesn't lead anywhere good. It hardens our hearts further and makes us even more vulnerable to temptation, moving us further from Christ.

Or maybe we become fixated on our shame. Conviction is positive; it draws us to repentance. The feeling of guilt we have when we are sinning is God-created so that we will turn back to Him and stop the sin. Shame that makes us loathe ourselves, continually condemn ourselves, doesn't come from God. He never wants us to wallow in our weakness, believing we are doomed, so why even try? Let's look at I Corinthians 10:13 piece by piece.

"No temptation has overtaken you except something common to mankind."

When I was at my lowest, wanting to control my situation, and hopeless because things weren't changing, one of the things that made it tough was feeling alone. I felt God was asking too much of me, placing me in a tough situation. I felt isolated in my pain. But in reality, the pain, frustration, and temptation I was facing had been faced countless times before by others. I wasn't alone. And God wasn't taken by surprise by my situation. He wasn't shocked that I was tempted. Nothing I was facing was new to God or really to humanity.

"God is faithful, so He will not allow you to be tempted beyond what you are able."

That phrase might give you pause. "If God hadn't allowed me to be tempted beyond what I could bear, then why did I sin?" But we have to remember, He is talking to believers here. He is talking to people who are in Christ, so it isn't we who live, but Christ who lives in us (Galatians 2:20). The Christ who is in us is faithful and able to withstand anything. We are able, as long as we are relying on His strength and not our own.

"But with temptation will provide a way of escape so that you will be able to endure it."

When we think of war or battles, we may picture an epic scene with an army of thousands pouring down a hill, ready to crush the enemy. We might picture hand-to-hand combat or troops stealthily sneaking up on the enemy. But there is another strategic action in a battle that is often overlooked:
Retreat. Escape.
God offers us a way to escape. However, we don't always take it. What if Peter had asked God what to do before he decided to try to hang around where the crowd was waiting. What if after that first denial he'd had the sense to just leave?
Sometimes we fail to resist temptation because we don't take God's escape route. A complimentary colleague becomes an inappropriate relationship because instead of walking away, we continue the conversations or messages so that we can soak up the good feelings. We become intoxicated because instead of leaving the party, we chose to stay, so the cool crowd would accept us. We fudge on that math a bit or take a little extra from the till because we are too embarrassed to ask for financial help. We hurt someone with angry words instead of tabling a conversation because, doggonit, we're *right!*
God is faithful. He always provides a way to escape. Even if we've never taken the escape before. Even if we've already blown it. Even at our most vulnerable, He is strong in our weakness, and He is able to bear it for us.

Here are a couple of believers in the Bible who didn't take their escapes. What could they have done?

Samson kept going back to Delilah. He knew she wasn't good for him. And after finding himself tied up after she wheedled the first secret out of him, he knew he couldn't trust her. Cutting off contact with a manipulative woman would have been a great escape.

David should have fulfilled his duty as king and been on the battlefield. Absent that, the moment he saw Bathsheba bathing and felt attractions, he could have walked right back into the palace, spent some time with his actual wife, found something else to do, or written a Psalm crying out to God.

All the real, human people in the Bible faced temptation. Except for Jesus, you can be sure they all succumbed from time to time. Romans 3 makes it clear that all of us have sinned. And that temptation didn't disappear just because they were believers. We still have a sinful nature. We still live in a fallen world. Take a look at what Paul, who wrote more of the New Testament than anyone, had to say:

"We know that the law is spiritual; but I am unspiritual, sold as a slave to sin. I do not understand what I do. For what I want to do I do not do, but what I hate I do...For I do not do the good I want to do, but the evil I do not want to do—this I keep on doing...but I see another law at work in me, waging war against the law of my mind and making me a prisoner of the law of sin at work within me. What a wretched man I am! Who will rescue me from this body that is subject to death?" Romans 7:14-15, 19, 23-24, NASB

Can you feel Paul's lament? I know I can. This is Paul, who preached the gospel, made disciples, wrote epistles, and rejoiced in prison. He still struggled and grieved over sin, but he never stopped serving Christ as long as he had breath.

David remained a man after God's own heart even after Bathsheba and Uriah. God restored Samson's strength, and at the end of his life, God used him to destroy a room full of wickedness. We are no different. We have the same God, the same forgiveness, and the same calling. God provides each of us a way of escape and the Christ-given strength to endure. Even when we do "blow it," His grace is sufficient, and repentance to Him can restore our fellowship with Him.

Words from Living Water

1. When we read about the disciples, we discover each of them had their own personalities, attributes, and human frailties. Peter tended to be impulsive in speech and actions, Thomas had a season of doubt, Andrew brought others to Jesus, Matthew was a reformed tax collector, and John was the disciple Jesus loved. I know I can see some Peter and Thomas in myself. Which of the disciples do you most identify with?

2. After Jesus has risen, He has a very important conversation with Peter. He doesn't chasten Peter for denying Him. That is over. Instead, He asks Him an important question. Read John 21:15-17. Why do you think Jesus had this conversation? Why is it important?

3. In Acts, after Paul is transformed on the roads to Damascus, the early believers were still somewhat skeptical of him and even afraid of him. How did Paul deal with this? When we repent and turn back to Christ, sometimes those who know our past may doubt. What does God want us to do in response, based on Paul's example?

Chapter 6: Renewal of the Heart and Mind

In the fallout of our wrong choices, sometimes it seems daunting and "false" to begin our daily spiritual disciplines again. Even if you've been a Christian for many years, picking up God's Word again to study it, praying daily, and having a quiet time can be overwhelming.

In my case, I just didn't know what to read. I felt so unworthy to study and analyze God's Word. It felt forced and false to dig into God's Word with my sin so fresh in my mind. What could God possibly teach me with such a brittle, broken heart? Where do I even start?

I started with Psalm 119. The Psalms seemed like a good choice, since David had made some massive mistakes, and he tended to share all of his feelings, fears, and frustrations on the page. He recorded the good, the bad, and the ugly. If he could write the Psalms, surely I could read them. I chose Psalm 119 for two reasons. First, the entire Psalm focuses on God's Word, its truth, its protection, and its unchanging nature. That seemed like solid footing after wading through sinking sand. Second, it was long. It was so hard to know where to start. I figured if I picked a chapter with 176 verses, I would at least have some time before I needed to figure out what to read next.

I cannot tell you how transformative it was to study that psalm as I began trying to live "after the well." I wrote my thoughts in a notebook when I could, and many days all I did was copy verses word for word out of the Psalm. Then I read them over and over. As I rebuilt the discipline of studying God's Word, I felt the weight lighten and my focus shift. Romans 12:2 tells us to "be transformed by the renewing of our minds," and God's Word is the foundation for that transformation.

After I finished Psalm 119, I wanted to read something in the New Testament. I craved practical, direct instructions. I'm convinced the stress of disobeying and hardening our hearts so ravages our minds, we need to go back to the basics and rebuild. So I decided to read through Galatians, Ephesians, Philippians, and Colossians.

Do you know why I chose those books? It wasn't some deep, profound epiphany or a voice that parted the clouds. No. It was the memory of something one of my former youth leaders said, He referred to those four books as the "General Electric Power Company" of our Christian lives. It was a clever phrase that used the first letter of each book's name. It sounded good to me because I definitely needed to be recharged.

I spent a lot of time reading the commands and promises in light of the immediate. There were things I knew I needed to do and repair. There were things in my mind and heart that needed serious realignment. Reading 176 verses in Psalms followed by the energy from the "General Electric Power Company" was exactly what my heart and mind needed.

You don't have to follow my plan. The important thing is opening God's Word again daily. Even if all you can do is copy verses or read them aloud. Even if you can only make it through a few verses at a time. It is vital for mental and spiritual renewal and reset. While this is just my opinion, as nice as audio Bibles are, they are passive. Our minds can easily wander while the audio becomes background noise. Once the verse has been read, it is gone. I encourage you to actually read the Bible with your own eyes. It will keep you more focused.

If reading the Bible seemed daunting, daily prayer was even harder to begin. I asked myself, how do I begin talking to the

One I ignored and rebelled against for so long? Confession made sense, of course, but how in the world could I praise Him? How could I ask for anything? And while confession is essential, prayer is not meant to be a constant exercise in self-flagellation. Telling God how sorry I was over and over when He had already forgiven me wasn't necessary, nor was I really doing it for *Him*. It was for me. It was at best a way to loathe myself and at worst performance, so He would know "I meant it." He forgave me the moment I came to Him in true repentance. Everything after was akin to vain repetition and mired in the idea I had that I needed to feel sufficiently terrible.

Understand, I am not minimizing the seriousness of sin. We should grieve over our sin. It should break our hearts. But again, remember the woman at the well. She didn't lie on the ground and moan or throw herself over the side of the well in a grand display of penance. Once she was freed, she had joy. Much of the display of self-condemnation we feel we should have or expect from others is a response to our human emotions. When someone wrongs us, we want them to suffer. When we wrong someone, we feel we should suffer. But once we confess, repent, and make any amends possible, the expectation that we should become the main character in Nathaniel Hawthorne's *The Scarlet Letter* is unbiblical.

The pain we may feel over hurting someone and even the natural consequence of our sin is understandable. Being free of the eternal consequences doesn't exempt us from earthly ones. But that pain should serve a purpose, not paralyze us or be a symbol of someone's exacting of a pound of flesh. And it should be an impetus for prayer, not hiding. I remember praying these words:

Lord, I am hurting so much right now over how I hurt others and You. I can't take away their pain. I don't deserve their forgiveness. Lord, please comfort each person who suffered because of me. Bring them healing. And Lord, guide me as I seek to rebuild. Help me to have wisdom, compassion, and empathy. Show me the actions You want me to take. Please help me to lean on you and learn from You. Keep me close, Lord. Test my thoughts. Give me a hunger for Your Word. Change me, O God.

That is the heart attitude a repentant believer should have. I cannot think of a better start to a renewed prayer life than utter honesty with God and dependence on Him. Remember the story of the Pharisee and the tax collector. It wasn't the flowery, self-aggrandizing prayer of the Pharisee God heard. It was the humble, broken prayer of the tax collector: "God, have mercy on me, a sinner!"

If you don't know where to start, you might want to begin with Psalm 119. Or may you want to read through all the Psalms. I recently did this; David's honesty always comforts me. Or maybe reading through the gospels would be a good start. Reading over and over about the life of Jesus is beneficial, remember how He came to Earth, who He was, and what He willingly did for us. It might be tempting to just read a book, and there are wonderful books out there. But I recommend diving directly into God's Word. Even though this is a book I would like for people to read, if you have to choose between spending time reading my words and spending time reading His, He always wins. Always.

Words from Living Water

1. In this chapter, I shared how God's Word healed me, challenged me, and comforted me. Regular study of His Word is essential for our spiritual health. This week, pray about this. With God's guidance, create a plan to study through an entire book of his Word, taking notes as you read.

2. Prayer is just as essential as God's Word. Regular conversation with God creates intimacy with Him. If you have never kept a prayer journal, where you cry out to Him, list requests and intercessions, and mark down God's answers and work, I encourage you to begin doing so. As you continue to journal and then look back to see how faithful God has been, I believe it will energize you.

Nave/What Happens After the Well

Chapter 7: Surrender: How to Lose Control

"She's got control issues!"

When we think of someone who fits the above description, we may think of a domineering parent, a micromanaging boss, or an intrusive, controlling spouse. Those types of people definitely fit the description. If you're a crime show buff like I am, you know profilers often talk about criminals such as rapists or serial killers needing "power and control."

But those are all pretty severe and stark views of controlling people.

All of us struggle with the battle between our flesh and our spirit, what we may want and what God wants. Ultimately, we are struggling with control. Who will have control of our lives - us or God? When we strip away the emotions and shallow justifications, almost every struggle with a pattern of sin has an element of control involved. We all have control issues because we all want to control *something*.

"Not me! I don't want to be in charge of anything! I've already got too much on my plate; I can barely hold it all together."

Well, dear one, that sort of illustrates my point. I've been there too. When we go "off the rails," we are often desperate to do one or more of a few things:
- Control an outcome
- Control a need
- Control a relationship
- Control a perception

Think about it. Think about the people we have gotten to know so far in God's Word
- Sarah wanted to control an outcome and a need
- Samson wanted to control a relationship and a perception
- Paul wanted to control outcomes and perceptions
- Naomi and her husband wanted to control a need
- Peter wanted to control an outcome and a perception
- David...well, I think David's answer would be all of the above!

The need or desire to control is the best friend of pride and fear, and it's one of the gifts that keeps on giving when we're born with a sinful nature. Sounds pretty dismal when we put it that way.

But...for believers...

We have wonderful promises, not the least of which we saw in I Corinthians 10:13 a couple of chapters ago. God always provides a way of escape, even from the temptation to take control. As long as we allow *Him* to be in control. And that is the key. How do we give up the control we cling to and give it to God Almighty? How do we lose control and surrender to Him?

I believe there are five components of surrender that we need to understand and apply in order to give God unconditional control of our lives:
- Humility before God
- Submission under God
- Sacrifice for God
- Contentment in God
- Intimacy with God

This chapter is pretty scripture-heavy, and I encourage you to take note of verses or passages that the Holy Spirit uses to prick your heart. These are great verses to memorize and meditate on so that His words are hidden in your heart. Both Psalm 1 and Joshua 1:8 encourage us to meditate on God's Word day and night.

Humility before God

Let's start with humility. We all know its opposite - pride. But sometimes we get a little stuck on what humility actually *is*. Here's what it is not: self-hatred, insecurity, self-deprecation, low self-esteem, and denial of our gifts and talents. Thinking I'm terrible isn't humility. It's a kind of pride because the focus is on us. I have known people who were constantly down on themselves or who brushed off all encouragement and compliments. That wasn't humility because they were still thinking of themselves, just in a negative light. When someone has godly humility, they see themselves in relation to Christ, and their focus is on Christ. And because they know they have become the righteousness of God through Christ, they certainly do not disparage what God redeemed.

Study the verses below to learn more about humility.

"But He gives a greater grace…Therefore it says, "God is opposed to the proud, but gives grace to the humble."…Humble yourselves in the presence of the Lord, and He will exalt you."
James 4:6, 10

In chapter 4, James placed these verses amid admonishments about quarreling, being selfish, being friends with the world, and mistreating our brothers and sisters in Christ. When people are focused on themselves, they become selfish, thoughtless, and often critical. Their priorities are out of whack. When we see ourselves in relation to God, we value what He values. This is part of having the "mind of Christ," which we'll talk about in a few paragraphs.

God is pretty clear about pride. He is opposed to it. In Proverbs 6, the writer lists seven things that God hates, and haughty eyes are listed first - *before* a lying tongue, a heart that devises wickedness, and hands that shed innocent blood. That's pretty serious. God is absolutely opposed to the proud.

But look at the next phrase: "He gives grace to the humble." Grace: the most valuable commodity in all the universe and eternity. When we are humble, God gives us grace. And not just grace. The beginning of that verse says he gives greater grace.

A few verses down, he reiterates another promise. When we humble ourselves, He will exalt us. In I Peter 5:6, it says "He will exalt you in due time." God will exalt us and show His glory through us when we get out of the way. Think of all the times the writers of the Old Testament and Paul refer to the people glorifying God because of His children. "They will see your works and glorify God." Jesus tells us the first shall be last and the last shall be first. Humility is a prerequisite to surrender.

Since I've already mentioned it, let's look more closely at I Peter 5:6-10. This is how humility is to play out in our lives.

To whom do we humble ourselves? Under the mighty hand of God. Remember, humility isn't about going around with shoulders slumped, thinking about how low we are. It's about who we are concerning God and how He sees us. Our focus is on His lordship.

What must we surrender to do this? In short, everything. Including the things that make us anxious, our fears, those things we think we desperately need, and all our cares. And that can feel scary.

When I was very small, I was playing with a doll, and somehow the side of her rubbery plastic head caved in, a bit like a rubber ball might. My grandfather loved telling this story because I came to him and said, "PaPa, my doll has a *pwobwem (problem)*." He told me he could fix it, but I'd have to let go and hand it to him. I needed to trust him. The doll was already injured. If I gave up holding onto her, I'd need to trust that PaPa could take care of her. Since I knew he loved me, I handed the doll to PaPa immediately.

We can trust God. He loves us infinitely more than my PaPa could ever love me, and that's saying something! Verse 7 tells us to "cast our cares on Him because He cares for us."

What are the warnings about my thoughts? Remember, when we have cares or anxieties, they can make us vulnerable. Verse 8 of James 4 warns us to be "sober in spirit." Then it goes on to say, "be alert!" Why do we need to be sober, alert, on guard? "Because our adversary, the devil, prowls around like a roaring lion, seeking whom he may devour." (NASB) Satan wants to devour us, and he is persistent and just plain crafty. So we cannot be passive.

How can I face such a challenge? We resist the devil, and that comes from being firm in our faith. We decide God will win by choosing our focus. And though this battle might seem lonely, verse 9 says we are not alone. The same experiences of suffering are being accomplished by our brothers and sisters in Christ.

How does it end? This is another promise from God: after we have suffered a little while, the God of all grace perfects us, confirms us, strengthens us, and establishes us. In due time, we are not just vindicated, we are exalted by the God who called us.

Honestly, when speaking of humility, John the Baptist said it best:

"He must increase, but I must decrease." John 3:30, NASB

That is the crux of biblical humility - God increases in us, and we decrease. More of Jesus, less of us.

Submission under God

Submission has to be one of the most misunderstood and maligned words in the Bible. When used in conjunction with marriage, it can spark sheer outrage among some groups. The theme of submission is repeated throughout God's Word, however, and it is the underpinning for the two greatest commandments found in Matthew 22:36-40. However, somehow we have incorrectly associated submission with weakness.

Submission may be many things, but it is absolutely not weak. Submission is not just a lazy, blind relinquishing of all our will or becoming a moldable jellyfish. Godly submission is a choice that involves trust, humility, and deep love, and those things require immense strength. When we submit to God, we can be sure those features are securely placed. God is imminently trustworthy, and he is deserving of our steadfast love. And we have already discussed what humility means in relation to God.

A few of the verses we've already explored speak of submission, which makes sense. One of these is found in James 4:7: "Submit yourselves therefore to God. Resist the devil and he will flee from you." NASB. This command comes just after James said God opposes the proud but gives grace to the humble. When we humble ourselves and receive His grace, then submitting to Him is the natural response.

So why should we submit to Christ? **First, because of our position in relation to Christ.** Well, that is part and parcel of claiming Him as the Lord of our lives. Lord, simply put, means boss. But it goes even deeper. He is our Master. And when we believe in Him, we become dead to self. He is to be the director of our lives. In addition, verse 7 tells us to resist the devil. It is impossible to resist the devil if we refuse to submit to Christ. Oh, we may be able to white-knuckle temptation for a while, but we are fallible. We have a sinful nature. When God is in charge and can guide our lives unhindered, He gives us the strength to resist. Satan is no match for God.

Second, **because of Christ's ownership**. I Corinthians 6:19-20 is one of my favorite reminders. It brings who we are and whose we are into sharp focus:

> "Or do you not know that your body is a temple of the Holy Spirit within you, whom you have from God, and that <u>you are not your own? For you have been bought for a price</u>: therefore glorify God in your body." NASB

Jesus paid the full price for our sins - for us. When we commit our lives to Him and accept that priceless gift, we become His. He owns us because He paid for us. Paul and others write about being slaves to Christ, and that is what we are. Unlike the cruel and shameful human version of slavery, which is unconscionable, being a slave to Christ is actually where true freedom lies. And God is supremely loving and faithful as our Lord.

Third, **we submit because we agreed to be His slaves.** In the human history of slavery, the victims are given no choice. They are ripped from their homes and families and sold to strangers who mistreat them. Sometimes they are even sold by family members, just like what happened to Joseph. When we become slaves to Christ, it is because we have chosen to follow Him. And unlike human slave owners, God will never abuse, mistreat, or neglect us. He draws us, and when we respond, we are saying yes to His ownership. Let's look at Romans 6:16:

"Do you not know that the one to whom you present yourselves as slaves for obedience, you are slaves of that same one whom you obey, either of sin resulting in death, or of obedience resulting in righteousness?" NASB

In the 1970s, Bob Dylan wrote a song called "Gotta Serve Somebody." The theme of that song is that all of us serve someone. Bob even got it right, according to Romans 6:16 As he sang, "It may be the devil, or it may be the Lord..." ("Gotta Serve Somebody," by Bob Dylan, from *Slow Train Coming*, 1979)

Bob was right, just like Paul was right. We choose. And when we choose Christ, we choose complete submission to Him. The good news is that when we serve as Christ's obedient servants, we inherit life and righteousness instead of death and destruction. I know which master I would rather serve!

Another reason we are to submit to Christ is that **we love Jesus**. It's that simple.

"If you love Me, you will keep My commandments." John 14:15, NASB

Jesus gives us the clearest test and confirmation of our love for Him in that verse: obedience. Not emotion, not tears, not a show on Sunday, not flowery words. Obedience. And we must remember that the coin of obedience has two slides:
- Doing what He said to do
- Not doing what He said Not to do

We've shunned that second one in our modern society. "Don't" has become a dirty word; a word our flesh calls "intolerant." But God's don'ts are not outdated or intolerant, they are unchanging, holy absolutes. Remember who Jesus is, according to John 1 - He is The Word. We cannot skirt around sin by saying, "Well, Jesus never mentioned *that*..." If God's Word mentioned it, Jesus did, because he is The Word. The Word was with God, and the Word was God. Jesus' commands involve the entirety of God's Word, not just the red letters printed by a binding company.

Finally, we submit to God **because submission means rest.** I love the verse below:

"Take My yoke upon you and learn from Me, for I am gentle and humble in heart, and you will find rest for your souls." Matthew 11:29

When we think of being servants or slaves, rest is the last word that usually comes to mind. From the Israelites in Egypt to the terrible era of slavery in the US, to the places around the world where slavery still exists, emotional and physical exhaustion are the norm. But then, Jesus is not the typical Master.

Jesus tells us in Matthew 11:30 that His yoke is easy, and His burden is light in the King James Version. When we submit our lives to Christ, we find more rest and more peace. Slavery to Christ, as I mentioned above, actually means freedom. Freedom from guilt, regret, shame, doubt, fear, and feeling lost. Freedom from the anxiety that comes from trying to figure out life all alone. Because He knows the plans He has for us, we can rest in Him. He will always do what is best. He is perfect.

Sacrifice for God

My Aunt Jean and Uncle Jim Livingston were career missionaries. They served in Vietnam, Malaysia, and the Philippines. While they were serving near Subic Bay, they led many to Christ from their refugee church. However, they did not baptize these new believers immediately. Instead, the new believers first went through a class regarding their new faith in Christ.

Here is why: Because of where they were and because of the circumstances these new converts were coming from, my aunt and uncle wanted to make sure they understood the commitment they were making. They wanted to be certain the people knew what surrender to Christ really meant. They didn't want to baptize someone who didn't fully understand salvation and might be just looking for an escape or wanting to please the American missionaries. Many of the people they reached were waiting to come to the US. Honestly, I think this is a wise thing to do in general. The church has used the idea of escaping Hell or the "sinners prayer" to unintentionally minimize what a true commitment to Christ involves. Not because we must work to earn salvation, but because there is more to the Christian life than where we go when we die. Surrender to Christ means sacrifice.

"Therefore I urge you, brothers and sisters, by the mercies of God, to present your bodies as a living and holy sacrifice, acceptable to God, which is your spiritual service of worship." Romans 12:1, NASB

In other words, our response to the ultimate sacrifice God in His mercy made when he allowed Jesus to be the sacrifice for us, we should offer ourselves as living sacrifices. And I love the final phrase: which is your spiritual act of worship. We've changed the meaning of worship to indicate the section of a church service or singing, or an emotion. True worship is being a living sacrifice for Christ every day. True worship is sacrifice. Let's answer some questions about sacrifice.

What do we give up?

When we sacrifice something, we give it up. That is what God did with His Son. However, God doesn't expect us to literally give the physical lives of our children like He did (though we should give them to God to do whatever He has planned for them). For one thing, our children aren't perfect like Jesus. So what does God ask us to give up?

"So then, none of you can be My disciple who does not give up all his own possessions." Luke 14:33, NASB

God does want us to be good stewards and not lay up treasures on earth. This, however, is about giving up all we have been and all we hold dear. The passage tells us that our love for and our commitment to Jesus should be so strong, our love for our families should look like hate in comparison (verse 26). This sacrifice for Christ was modeled perfectly by Christ. Take a look at Philippians 2:5-8.

"Have this attitude in yourselves which was also in Christ Jesus, who, as He already existed in the form of God, did not consider equality with God something to be grasped, but emptied Himself by taking the form of a bond-servant and being born in the likeness of men. And being found in appearance as a man, He humbled Himself by becoming obedient to the point of death: death on a cross." NASB

Look at the attributes in these verses. He didn't consider equality with God something to be grasped. Jesus actually *was* God in the flesh. However, He didn't cling to that position. We are not equal to God, so we certainly shouldn't try to cling to any illusion of grandeur, and we shouldn't cling to our own position as god in our lives. Jesus emptied Himself by taking on the form of a bondservant. This harks back to submission; He submitted completely to His Father and His Father's plan. Emptying oneself is such a powerful picture here as well.

Then He became obedient to the point of death. I encourage you to read Hebrews 12:2-4 when you have a chance. It talks about what Jesus did and admonishes us as well. There were no limits to Jesus's obedience to His Father. Can we say the same? I know for myself, I am guilty of singing "I surrender all," when what I lived was "I surrender some." Sometimes the harder things are a struggle:

- Giving, even when finances are tight
- Turning the other cheek, even if we want vengeance
- Working as unto the Lord, even when the boss is a jerk

- Forgiving, even when it really hurt
- Standing for our belief in Christ, even if there are social consequences

There was nothing Jesus wouldn't sacrifice if His Father willed it, even His life.

What do we have to lose?

"For whoever wants to save his life will lose it, but whoever loses his life for My sake and the gospel's will save it." Mark 8:35, NASB

It's true, the stakes are high when it comes to surrendering our lives to Christ. It isn't just life or death on earth; it is infinitely bigger than that. When we choose self over God regarding salvation, the consequences are eternal. As Christians who are in Him, our eternity will be in Heaven. However, when we try to cling to the temporal over the eternal, we lose the impact we could have for Him, we lose the joy we have when we give our lives in His service, and we lose the opportunity to make an eternal difference in the lives of others.

Jim Elliot, a missionary who was martyred in Ecuador, said something very profound: "He is no fool who gives what he cannot keep to gain what he cannot lose." This life and all that we gain in it will come to an end. We will never be able to hold onto the things, feelings, and pleasures we have in this world. So it makes sense to prioritize the eternal over the temporary. The wise course of action is to sacrifice what we cannot keep in order to focus on what matters for eternity.

What do we have to take up?

"And He was saying to them all, 'If anyone wants to come after Me, he must deny himself, take up his cross daily, and follow Me.'" Luke 9:23, NASB

What does it mean to take up our cross? In Roman times, when someone was crucified, they often had to carry their own cross. Somewhere along the line, we equated cross-bearing with a burden or grief or unchangeable feature: "It's just my cross to bear." Taking up our cross daily is not about resigning ourselves to some horrible fate and bearing it as best we can. Taking up our cross means bearing whatever we need to follow Christ. Removing it as an obstacle in our path. Yes, it may be situationally different for everyone. It might be an addiction for some, a history of trauma for others, or a cycle of poverty for others. And it can change. For many years, the loneliness of being invisible in my own home became the cross I eventually refused to take up. When that happens, that obstacle can cause us to stumble into the abyss.

Galatians 2:20 illuminates this a bit. It says, "I have been crucified with Christ; and it is no longer I who live, but Christ lives in me; and the life which I now live in the flesh I live by faith in the Son of God, who loved me and gave Himself up for me" (*NASB*). Being crucified with Christ means we have died to self. When we willingly crucify ourselves, we ultimately sacrifice all of our "rights." That is a radical concept, especially in a time when the idea of rights has permeated every discussion and every situation. As Christians, the only right we actually have - spiritually speaking - is the right to die to self and live for Christ.

Sacrifice is a pretty heavy concept. But it is a necessary component of biblical surrender.

Contentment in Christ

It's hard to surrender in a situation or environment where we are needy, uncomfortable, anxious, or frustrated. Our nature is to act to change that environment, try to escape it, or try to compensate somehow. For example, I know a couple who adopted a toddler from a foreign country. The orphanage was in a poor country, and the children there had very little. The new little family bonded quickly, and the little girl seemed happy in her new home. However, she constantly wanted to eat. Even if it was clear she was not actually hungry, she wanted to eat and eat until she was sick. She had lived without enough food, and now she was afraid the food would go away, so she ate as much as she could.

This phenomenon is common in many children and adults who have experienced long-term food insecurity. Similarly, people who grew up during the depression are more likely to "hoard" things. When an elderly family member died several years ago, we helped clean out the house. There were hundreds of butter tubs, twist ties, and other things in her kitchen. She grew up during the depression, and she couldn't bear to throw things away that might be useful. We also found buttons, fabric remnants, and all sorts of other items throughout the house. After growing up with nothing, she held onto everything.

Contentment, that place of peace regardless of circumstances, is at its core a matter of trust. If we do not trust God to take care of us and we do not have Him as our source of peace, we will be discontent. And it isn't just about whether or not we believe He is able. Many years ago, during a time of great loneliness, disillusionment, and sadness, I went through a study on the book of Habakkuk. One of the study questions asked if we believed God was able to provide for us completely. I remember writing that I absolutely believed God *could* provide what I needed; I just didn't believe He *would*. You see, I had prayed fervently that God would change some painful things, and He hadn't done that. I can look back and see how I allowed my heart to begin blaming God, hardening, in that simple statement. I was discontent.

Let's look at a passage in Matthew chapter 6:

"For this reason, I say to you, do not be worried about your life, as to what you will eat or what you will drink; nor for your body, as to what you will put on. Is life not more than food, and the body more than clothing? Look at the birds of the sky, that they do not sow, nor reap, nor gather crops into barns, and yet your heavenly Father feeds them. Are you not much more important than they? And which of you by worrying can add a single day to his life's span? And why are you worried about clothing? Notice how the lilies of the field grow; they do not labor nor do they spin thread for cloth, yet I say to you that not even Solomon in all his glory clothed himself like one of these. But if God so clothes the grass of the field, which is alive today and tomorrow is thrown into the furnace, will He not much more clothe you? You of little faith! Do not worry then, saying, 'What are we to eat?' or 'What are we to drink?' or 'What are we to wear for clothing?' For the Gentiles eagerly seek all these things; for your heavenly Father knows that you need all these things. But seek first His kingdom and His righteousness, and all these things will be provided to you.

"So do not worry about tomorrow; for tomorrow will worry about itself. Each day has enough trouble of its own." v. 25-34

I love this passage. In the Spring, I enjoy taking walks to see the flowers blooming. From those first cherry blossoms to the azaleas and dogwoods, to all the perennials and bulb flowers that fill the world with color, I fill my phone with images. And these are just fragile plants that fade after a season. We are made in God's image and have an eternal spirit. We are infinitely more important than a flower.

I also love the line, *for your heavenly Father knows that you need all these things.* Jesus knows exactly what we need, and as Philippians 4:19 says, He supplies them all according to His riches. We can have peace that He will take care of us. We can be content in that knowledge.

In a similar vein, take a look at Philippians 4:6-7:

"Do not be anxious about anything, but in everything by prayer and pleading with thanksgiving let your requests be made known to God. And the peace of God, which surpasses all comprehension, will guard your hearts and minds in Christ Jesus." NASB

When I was thirty, I had some routine day surgery. It was intended to be laparoscopic (only a tiny incision). However, the surgeon saw two pretty significant tumors. One was clearly benign, but the other was suspicious. I would have to wait for biopsy results. Honestly, I didn't think I was worried at first. Then, once the anesthesia faded, it really hit me. I had a baby and a toddler. The "what ifs" sent me into severe anxiety, and I couldn't seem to stop the fearful scenarios from running through my mind. I cried out to God, and immediately Philippians 4:6-7 came to mind. I felt God's comfort.

Laurie, don't be anxious about this. Instead, call on me, give it to me, request to me. My peace that passes understanding is ready to guard your heart and mind.

Immediately, I was at peace. I still didn't have the lab results, but my mind was quieted, and my heart was still. The Psalms are full of exhortations to cry out to God and rest in Him. I won't type them all out, but I encourage you to read these when you need God's peace:

- Psalm 46:1
- Psalm 46:10
- Psalm 23
- Psalm 37:4
- Psalm 4:8

When it comes to contentment, Philippians 4:10-13 gets down to brass tacks. Look at what he says here:

"But I rejoiced in the Lord greatly, that now at last you have revived your concern for me; indeed, you were concerned before, but you lacked an opportunity to act. Not that I speak from need, for I have learned to be content in whatever circumstances I am. I know how to get along with little, and I also know how to live in prosperity; in any and every circumstance I have learned the secret of being filled and going hungry, both of having abundance and suffering need. I can do all things through Him who strengthens me." NASB

In this passage, Paul is referring to his financial well-being. In his ministry and travels, sometimes Paul received generous gifts. Sometimes he barely had enough to continue. This is what he means when he talks about knowing the secret of having abundance and of suffering need. Verse 11 tells us Paul *learned to be content* in whatever his circumstances were. It didn't come naturally. Paul had to *learn* how to be content in Christ. And once he did, he could rejoice and have peace no matter what was or wasn't in his wallet. Paul was content because his security didn't come from his financial situation. It came from Christ. That is why he said, "I can do all things through Him who strengthens me."

This might seem like nonsense. I know there were seasons in my life where I worried about how to buy groceries or how to have the electricity turned on again. I wish I could say I was like Paul - content and unworried. Sometimes I was, but sometimes I worried, pouted, and eventually did what Sarah did. I figured out a way to fix it myself. And my ways were definitely *not* God's.

That brings me to another set of verses that are useful to memorize:

> "Trust in the Lord with all your heart
> And do not lean on your own understanding.
> In all your ways acknowledge Him,
> And He will make your paths straight."
> Proverbs 3:5-6

One of the main reasons we need to surrender to Christ is the fallibility of our own understanding. David got it right; the heart is desperately wicked. Like Matthew 7 says, our understanding is shifting sand, unable to withstand even the simplest storm. Jesus Christ and His Word are the bedrock that never moves.

Build your house on that bedrock, and you will experience peace and contentment.

Intimacy with Christ

The word trust can be a trigger, especially for those in pain either because of others' actions or our own choices. It's devastating when we realize we can no longer trust someone we love. And when the person we cannot trust is ourselves, we feel lost.

The hard truth in this life is that we really *can't* trust ourselves. We are all fallible, with a sinful nature. As the hymn says, we are "prone to wander...prone to leave the God I love." Just look at the endless cycle of the children of Israel. Even Paul couldn't trust himself, as we saw in Romans 7.

But Jesus? We can trust Him implicitly and without reservation. Jesus never fails. Our problem is that we sometimes don't believe we can trust Him. Or perhaps we worry that He won't deal with our circumstances in the way we want Him to - the way *we* would.

Maybe we just don't know Him well enough. In our human relationships, it's hard to fully trust someone we don't really know. On the other hand, in our closest relationships, trust grows with intimacy. I trust my husband. I trust my parents. I trust my lifelong friend, Belinda.

The more intimacy we have with Christ, the more we understand His ways and His faithfulness. The longer we walk with Him, the more examples we have of His goodness. Lamentations 3 says "this I recall to mind, therefore I have hope…" And when we deeply commune with Him, the more we become like Him. And that also means obedience to Him. Paul understood how important it was to truly know Christ. It was his deepest desire.

"But whatever things were gain to me, these things I have counted as loss because of Christ. More than that, I count all things to be loss in view of the surpassing value of knowing Christ Jesus my Lord, for whom I have suffered the loss of all things, and count them mere rubbish, so that I may gain Christ, and may be found in Him, not having a righteousness of my own derived from the Law, but that which is through faith in Christ, the righteousness which comes from God on the basis of faith, that I may know Him and the power of His resurrection and the fellowship of His sufferings, being conformed to His death; if somehow I may attain to the resurrection from the dead." Philippians 3:7-11, NASB

Before Paul was redeemed on the road to Damascus, he was considered by the Jewish community to be part of the religious elite - a Hebrew of Hebrews. He had a lot he could have boasted about and the credentials to back up his claims. In addition, he was likely fairly wealthy when he was still a Pharisee. Like the Beatles' song says, he was a "well-respected man about town." But, in verse 8, he says he considers all of those things loss. He actually calls them dung. If you've ever been to a zoo and smelled camel dung, you know what a drastic statement that is!

When Paul said he wanted to know Christ, he meant *all* of knowing Christ: the power of His resurrection, the fellowship of His sufferings, being conformed to Him in His death. Paul didn't just want to get loaves, fish, and healing. He was all in. He wanted the biblical version of knowing Christ. Our modern society embraces the more "hippie" version of Jesus, handing out blessings telling us "judge not," and "love your neighbor" (though the world gets those two phrases impressively wrong). But suffering, absolutes, crucifying self? No thank you. Paul wasn't looking for the easy road; he was looking for the holy one. He lived like Jesus, spoke like Jesus, and he suffered like Jesus. He was intimate with his Lord.

Colossians 3 gives us great insights into how to be intimate with Christ in a way that influences everything we do. The first two verses give us the key:

"Therefore, if you have been raised with Christ, keep seeking the things that are above, where Christ is, seated at the right hand of God. Set your minds on the things that are above, not on the things that are on earth." NASB

Again, we see the direction our focus should take. Our minds should be set on Him. As Hebrews 12:2, we should fix our eyes on Jesus, the author and perfecter of our faith. Our minds, our affections, and our focus should be set on things above. He should be the primary relationship of our hearts.

When we make knowing Him the priority, something wonderful happens. We adopt His mind and His desires. We seek Him more and more, and we worry about the world less and less.

"Delight yourself in the Lord; and He will give you the desires of your heart."
Psalm 37:4, NASB

We must understand what that last part is *not* saying. This verse is not a transaction - I'll delight in You, God, and You'll give me what I want. This verse is a *transformation*. As we delight in Him, He conforms our desires to His desires. He shows us what we *should* desire - which is what He desires for us. That was something I missed, unintentionally. It wasn't conscious, but I realized when my life didn't go the way I thought it would, I had assumed that since I did things the "right" way, certain aspects of my life would certainly be happy or easy. I was a bit put out when that didn't happen; I struggled in areas I thought would be joyful and fulfilling. Had I fully understood this verse, I wouldn't have been so caught off guard by suffering and disappointment.

    Intimacy with God makes us like Him. We know His heart and mind, and when we do, we are more than willing to surrender to such a Savior.

    When we humble ourselves, when we submit to God, when we are willing to sacrifice and find our contentment in Him, and when we are truly intimate with Him, surrender is natural. And a surrendered life is an abundant life.

Words from Living Water

Each day this week, review the verses we have discussed for each of the different aspects of surrender, and meditate on the following questions:

- Humility before God
- Submission under God
- Sacrifice for God
- Contentment in God
- Intimacy with God

1. How does God's Word define today's aspect? What does it look like?

2. As you meditate on humility, submission, sacrifice, contentment, and intimacy, how is God directing you to surrender to Him? Are there things in your life that need to be moved aside or changed in order to exhibit these traits of surrender?

3. Choose a verse to add to your Scripture memory list that addresses each of these aspects. God says we are to hide His Word in our hearts, meditate on them day and night. List the reference below.

Chapter: 8 Choosing Our Circle

As I review my life and its ups and downs - especially spiritually - I can see an interesting correlation. When I was the most diligent, disciplined, and consistent in my daily walk with Christ, I seemed to also have a good support system of godly Christian friends. And when I isolated myself or just didn't have the opportunity to connect closely with other faithful believers, I was more vulnerable. Yes, we are all responsible for our own choices, and no one can sustain our fellowship with Christ except us. But when my circle pointed me toward Christ and walked alongside me in pursuing Him, both of us (or all of us) were more consistent on our day-to-day faith. This makes sense when we read Ecclesiastes:

"Two are better than one because they have a good return for their labor; for if either of them falls, the one will lift up his companion. But woe to the one who falls when there is not another to lift him up! Furthermore, if two lie down together they keep warm, but how can one be warm alone? And if one can overpower him who is alone, two can resist him. A cord of three strands is not quickly torn apart." Ecclesiastes 4:9-12, NASB

I love the image of a strong cord with several strands winding together. I remember seeing an illustration of this when I was young, and it's true. Even the thinnest, smallest cords become strong when they are woven together. I've seen the strength of multiple cords in my own life.

When I was in junior high school, my family joined a new church. The first night we visited, I met J, and we became fast friends. J had become a Christian a year before, and she was a passionate follower. She studied her Bible, had an ever-growing prayer list, and shared Jesus with almost everyone. J was 100% real through and through. Daily time with God and talk about our faith was woven into our friendship. I can't count the number of times we knelt beside the bed at one of our houses, praying through pages of requests and praising God for His blessings. I admit I couldn't always keep up with her energy. Sometimes I nodded off to sleep on the floor while she kept going.

My friendship with J endured through the years and decades until she died in 2011. She had a profound, lasting impact on my life. Her faithfulness, honesty, and loving challenges helped carry me through several dark seasons.

God's Word has quite a bit to say about the benefits of godly friends. Let's look at a few:

"Oil and perfume make the heart glad, And a person's advice is sweet to his friend."
Proverbs 27:9, NASB

This tells me that part of the sweetness of a real friendship is loving truth-telling. That point is important because there is a vast difference between an unconditional cheerleader and a faithful, godly friend. Consider these verses:

"As iron sharpens iron, So one person sharpens another." Proverbs 27:17, NASB
"Better is open rebuke than love that is concealed. Faithful are the wounds of a friend, but deceitful are the kisses of an enemy." v. 5-6

An unconditional cheerleader who agrees with all our choices, backs all our opinions, and agrees with everything we do may make us feel warm and fuzzy. But they do not necessarily make the best or wisest friends. A friend with true agape love for us will speak up when we are headed down a destructive path. It's like the difference between cotton candy and hearty vegetables. The cotton candy is pretty and tastes sweet, but it has no substance. Vegetables give us strength and health. Let's take a closer look at God's design for friendship:

- "And let's consider how to encourage one another in love and good deeds." Hebrews 10:24, NASB
- "But speaking the truth in love, we are to grow up in all aspects into Him who is the head, that is, Christ." Ephesians 4:15, NASB
- "A friend loves at all times, and a brother is born for adversity." Proverbs 17:17, NASB
- "This is My commandment, that you love one another, just as I have loved you. Greater love has no one than this, that a person will lay down his life for his friends." John 15:12-13, NASB

We often think of friends as pals to socialize with, laugh with, enjoy hobbies with, etc. And there is nothing wrong with those things. Enjoying life with people we care about is a blessing. But like everything else, Jesus wants our friendships to have a purpose. Like the twelve men He walked with and taught (and the three He was closest with), we are to walk together toward God's will, God's Word, and God's plan. The amazing thing about godly Christian friendships that distinguish them from social connections or partners in fun is the fact that Christian friendships can be eternal. When my lifetime friend died in 2011, I grieved. I still do at times. However, I am going to see her again. When we both are with Jesus, we will worship and serve Him forever.

Hebrews 10:24-25 is as follows:

"And let's consider how to encourage one another in love and good deeds, not abandoning our own meeting together, as is the habit of some people, but encouraging one another; and all the more as you see the Day drawing near." NASB

What does it mean to encourage one another in love and good deeds? Sometimes it's helpful to take a look at other translations:
- NIV Bible - "spur one another on"
- NLT Bible - "think of ways to motivate one another"
- ESV Bible - "stir up one another"
- KJV Bible - consider one another to provoke
- AMP Bible - "consider (thoughtfully) how we may encourage one another"
- Holman Bible - "be concerned about one another in order to promote"

(The above translations came from www.biblehub.com)

In this case, all those words - spur on, motivate, provoke, etc. paint a picture of support, engagement, and exhortation. And if you notice the KJV and Holman examples, they say, "consider one another" and "be concerned about one another." Our love and concern for our brothers and sisters in Christ should be our impetus for encouraging and motivating them.

How should we tell the truth in love? Ephesians 4 as a chapter talks a lot about how we interact with each other: with kindness, without malice, tenderhearted, forgiving, truthful. When He tells us how to speak to our brothers and sisters, the command has two parts - tell the truth & in love.

Strangely, Christians too often seem to see this two-part command as two separate camps - the love camp and the truth camp. They create a dichotomy where there is none. God knows that one without the other is useless, frivolous, cruel, and out of balance. Let's explore the shortcomings of each of these camps.

The "tell the truth" camp

These campers are easy to spot, especially on social media. Not only is everything extreme black and white, tact is usually absent. When they are encouraged to add some love, they get defensive and respond, "That's just how I am. I tell it like it is," or "Some people just can't handle truth." Yes, the truth can be convicting, hard, and uncomfortable, but the way we choose to talk to people matters. This is the camp that likes to point to Jesus overturning the tables and John the Baptist calling Pharisees vipers in order to justify - well - being a jerk. Ironically, this camp actually has more in common with the Pharisees to whom John the Baptist was referring.

The "love" camp
The love camp seems nicer and more innocuous. They wrap you in more hugs, ease your hurt, and emphasize your entitlement to do and be whatever you desire. Authentic love is good, but this love is shallow. The problem with this unconditional approval of everything, is the danger of being so offended by black and white that they drown in the gray. I heard a preacher talk once about loving someone right into hell. That means they consider any confrontation about sin or declaring something sin at all to be unloving. But the God who loves us also demands holiness and cannot fellowship with sin. Real love understands this.

Telling the truth in love means we love others enough to tell them God's truth and, like Hebrews 10:24 says, encourage them to live that truth. But it also means we lovingly share that truth. Patting our sister on the back as she lives out what God declares to be a sin is not love, but neither is calling her terrible or dirty or ostracizing her.

This balance can be hard, but it is essential. Following the whole of Ephesians 4:15 may be painful at times for the giver and the receiver. But remember what Proverbs says:

"Faithful are the wounds of a friend, but deceitful are the kisses of an enemy." Proverbs 27:6, NASB

When I was rebelling against God, I had two friends who were professing Christians. Now, understand, my wrong choices were mine alone. I was the one responsible to turn back to God; it was not someone else's responsibility to turn me. However, I'd like to illustrate the truth of these verses. I shared my struggle with a friend I'll call Patty. She didn't exactly cheer me on. She shrugged a bit and told me it wasn't her place to judge. By the way, that is not biblical. It absolutely *is* our responsibility to correctly assess sin and lovingly confront one another. At any rate, when I was on that terrible roller coaster of guilt, Patty suggested I just tell God I was sorry and forget about it. After all, it wasn't all my fault, right? Just lock it in the vault and move on.

After my heart was broken in that Kroger parking lot, I called another friend who I'll call Betty and poured out everything to her. She listened, murmured encouragement, and prayed with me. She told me she loved me. She also told me that my sin was sin. And she went further; she told me that hiding it was more sin. It was exactly what God would have told me had He been sitting in the car. And she was right.

Because Betty was willing to tell me the truth in love, the Holy Spirit used her words to spur me beyond just sobbing in my car and toward taking the first step in bearing the fruit of repentance. And Betty isn't the only friend who has done that for me. God has used other friends, my mother, and at one point my adult child to hold up a mirror and turn me from a destructive path. Yes, I didn't just trip once and then jump back on my golden cloud. My heart can be woefully stubborn. Maybe that's why characters like David and the many stories of the nation of Israel resonate with me.

Think about your circle. Who is in it, and how does that friendship or relationship compare to Christ's model? Do you have people in your life who will love you the way Jesus loves and point you toward Him? Are you that kind of friend to others? If not, is there someone you see in church, in school, or across the street who loves Jesus, someone you could reach out to? Maybe you feel uncomfortable reaching out. I can understand that. I had a large, energetic circle of Christian friends in high school and college. In my thirties, that circle dwindled somewhat. For part of my forties I had almost no real friendships, save those who lived far away. As we get older it seems harder to form the kind of open, vulnerable friendships we had when we were younger. But we need those.

Paul had Timothy, Peter had the other apostles. Mark, Barnabas, James, John...they all traveled in pairs or more as they shared the gospel. During Jesus's ministry, the women who walked with Jesus forged a bond, and they were with Mary at the crucifixion and walked together to the tomb. Even farther back: Job's friends visited him in his time of grief. Granted, sometimes they acted like jerks. But they were *there*. They loved their hurting brother.

As you walk closer to Christ, don't take the journey alone. Pray that God will connect you with someone who will sharpen you, tell you the truth, and motivate you to love and good deeds. Remember what Jesus said:

"By this all people will know that you are My disciples: if you have love for one another." John 13:35, NASB

Words from Living Water

1. Read Proverbs 27:17 and Hebrews 10:24. Based on these verses, what is a good friend to do with and for us?

2. Think about the friends you have. Are you the type of friend who will "tell the truth in love," or do you tend to keep the peace and avoid painful conversations, even when you see your friend walking down the wrong path?

3. Some people believe that identifying sin is "judging" and a sign that we do not love someone unconditionally. What do the Scriptures in this chapter teach us about that misconception?

4. Identify friends in your life who point you toward Christ. Be sure to thank them for helping you to follow Him. And if you do not have this kind of friend, ask God to bring someone into your life.

Chapter 9: Dealing with Doubt

I originally intended to title this chapter "Dealing with Doubters," meaning, "How do we deal with those who may doubt our sincerity, the change in our lives, or God's work in our lives after we fail?" But the more I thought about it and the more I studied, the more I realized a truth.

We don't "deal with" the doubters. God does. While we are accountable for our actions, we are called to take responsibility for our choices, and we should seek to make amends when possible; improving others' perception of us is neither our priority nor our job. Not really. That doesn't mean the people affected by our actions are not important. We should be sensitive, compassionate, and humble. But the woman at the well didn't try to "prove" she was different to make others in the town think more highly of her. Paul didn't try to do "damage control" or PR, explaining he only did those things when he was a Pharisee, though I am sure he told his story of conversion numerous times. His goal was not to convince people he had changed. That would mean the focus was on himself and what others thought. And as he said in Galatians 1:10:

"For am I now seeking the favor of men, or God? Or am I striving to please men? If I were still trying to please men, I would not be a bond-servant of Christ." (NASB)

So while we will discuss how to respond to those who may doubt the change in our lives, I believe - like Paul did - that our focus should be on following Christ faithfully. God will take care of the perceptions and thoughts of others.

In this chapter, we'll talk about how to deal with doubt - whether internal or external - using three tools/disciplines: Perseverance, Prayer, and Perspective.

Prayer

It's no accident that verses about perseverance often appear alongside verses about trials, hardships, and temptations. God uses these things to grow us. That is, *if* we allow Him to and if we purpose to keep our eyes focused on Him. If we keep our eyes fixed on Jesus, the author and *perfecter* of our faith When we do that, we can persevere through the storms, even the storms we helped create.

I read a lot and hear a lot of people say that we forget God in the good times and then run back to Him and cling to Him in the bad times. That can certainly be true when a loved one is ill or a tragedy occurs. For me, sometimes it is actually the opposite. I only cling to God in the rough times when I make a conscious choice to do so. I must admit that often, when things seem unfairly tough and especially when God doesn't seem to be moving quickly enough, my perseverance will flag and self-pity, impatience, and resentment creep in. When things go smoothly or relatively well, I may take it for granted, but I am thankful, and reading God's Word, praying, etc. seems easy. When I am faced with a storm I cannot control (smile), it is harder to focus because I just want God to do something about it.

That's why I am thankful God doesn't expect us to persevere on our own. In II Corinthians 12, Paul talks about his "thorn in the flesh." We don't know exactly what this is, despite scholars who have declared it to be one thing or another. I believe it isn't specified so that it is more easily applicable to whatever we are facing. Paul asked God several times to remove this thorn, and God chose not to do so. Here is what Paul said:

"And He (God) has said to me, 'My grace is sufficient for you, for power is perfected in weakness.' Most gladly, therefore, I will rather boast about my weaknesses, so that the power of Christ may dwell in me. Therefore I delight in weaknesses, in insults, in distresses, in persecutions, in difficulties, in behalf of Christ; for when I am weak, then I am strong." II Corinthians 12:9-10, NASB

Even amid an ongoing struggle, one that God wasn't going to just "fix," Paul persevered. He was even grateful for the weakness because it meant He could rest in God's strength.

In James 1;2-4, we are told the following:

"Consider it all joy, my brothers and sisters, when you encounter various trials, knowing that the testing of your faith produces endurance. And let endurance have its perfect result, so that you may be perfect and complete, lacking in nothing." James 1:2-4, NASB

James tells us to count it "joy" when we face trials because of the perseverance they produce. When we persevere, we can become perfect and complete, lacking in nothing. I know I would sure like to be that way! However, that isn't the end of what James says, and I am glad:

"But if any of you lacks wisdom, let him ask of God, who gives to all generously and without reproach, and it will be given to him."

Do you ever lack wisdom? I know for sure I do. And God's Word says that if we do, all we need to do is to ask God. Not only will He give us wisdom, but He also gives it generously, and He doesn't shame us for needing it. God doesn't roll His eyes and say, "Hasn't she learned *yet?*" He gives us the wisdom we need every time we ask.

James doesn't stop there either. In verse 12 he goes on to say that if we persevere under trial, we are blessed and we will "receive the crown of life which the Lord has promised to those who love Him." What an exciting promise!

Let's talk a bit about what this perseverance means with regard to those around us. When Paul had his Damascus Road experience, God told Ananias to go to him. Ananias was a bit skittish: "Are you sure, God?" He knew what Paul had done to believers. Even after Ananias went and was convinced of Paul's transformation, the other early believers were still skeptical. Can you blame them? This was the man who sought out and imprisoned believers. This was the man who stood by and held the cloaks of those who stoned their beloved friend, Stephen. Just because Paul had repented after Damascus didn't mean those things didn't happen.

Likewise, when people saw that Jesus was headed home with Zacchaeus, the chief tax collector, they were appalled: "Look! Jesus is going home with that thief who steals from us! Can you believe that?" The same thing happened when the woman anointed Jesus with expensive oil: "Does He know what kind of woman she is? And look at that waste! She should have given that to the poor!" Finally, think of the older brother in the story of the prodigal son. He had been faithful to his father for years, and when the black sheep finally comes home, they throw a party for him!

When we look at things from a distance, it might be easy to be impatient with a brother or sister who is holding onto someone's past bad actions. But remember, when someone rebels against God, they leave damage in their wake. We can forgive the sin, forgive the pain, but it is still there, at least in our memories. So what do we do when we have truly repented, God has restored fellowship with Him, and we are once again following Christ, but the gossips and skeptics are still shaking their heads?

I'll share an event from my own life. I am adopted and am enthusiastically pro-life. When my state was considering legislation that would further protect the most innocent of lives - the unborn - I was vocal on social media. It struck a nerve with a Facebook connection. She knew I had fallen in my life and made some sinful choices. She began commenting every time I posted about being pro-life, saying things like, "Isn't the sin of (insert) as bad as abortion?" or "At least I haven't done X. People want to protect a clump of cells but will happily do X!"

I ignored the first comment or two, praying about what to do. I couldn't call her a liar. She knew what I had done in my past. But as the comments became more and more caustic, I knew I needed to respond. After all, my children are also connected on FB, and while I had been honest with them as well, they didn't need to see that. I sent her a private message, telling her that she was right - I had made some terrible choices in the past. I told her it was never my intention to hurt her, and I apologized for triggering pain. She didn't answer and kept making remarks. Eventually, I blocked her and took down the posts with her comments. I didn't want to hide anything, but it was disruptive. I wasn't angry with her. But it did bring home once again that sin has consequences, humans have memories, and being sorry doesn't magically erase that.

A few years ago, I wrote a poem called "There Are Scars," and I'd like to share it with you:

There Are Scars
There are scars
When choices that we make cause pain for those we love
There are scars
That mark the wounds of those who suffered in our path
And even when
We see the light and our hearts break for all the damage we have done
And we repent
Still there are scars

He forgives
The sacrifice He made can wash away our sins
Oh He forgives
The only sinless one became the sin for all of us that day
But even when
The one who falls before Him humbly is a new creation now
And right with Him
Still there are scars

So let us seek….to heal the ones whose hearts
Were broken by……our selfishness and pride
And when our words and actions cannot turn the tide of time and pain
Still, let us pray….and then be changed
When there are scars

But there is hope
The hope of our new life that's given by His grace
There is hope
That in His name we can be used to share His love
And there is hope
That He's sufficient to bring healing if we seek to be made whole
And rest in Him
Even when
There are scars

When we repent, return to Christ, and follow Him, we cannot undo our wrong choices. God can heal *our* hearts. He is also the one who can heal the hearts of those who were *hurt*. Just like no one else can change us, we cannot force the healing of others. All we can do is what God has told us to do concerning sin. And it's human nature to define each other with a narrow view. Even Shakespeare knew this when he wrote:

"The evil that men do lives after them;
The good is oft interred with their bones"
Julius Caesar, William Shakespeare

Returning to what perseverance means for us, let's look at one of my favorite passages in Philippians 3. It comes after Paul talks about how nothing compares to the surpassing greatness knowing Christ.

"Not that I have already grasped it all or have already become perfect, but I press on if I may also take hold of that for which I was even taken hold of by Christ Jesus. Brothers and sisters, I do not regard myself as having taken hold of it yet; but one thing I do: forgetting what lies behind and reaching forward to what lies ahead, I press on toward the goal for the prize of the upward call of God in Christ Jesus." Philippians 3:12-14, NASB

This idea of laying aside and moving forward is echoed throughout God's Word. Take a look at Hebrews 12:1-2:

"Therefore, since we also have such a great cloud of witnesses surrounding us, let's rid ourselves of every obstacle and the sin which so easily entangles us, and let's run with endurance the race that is set before us, looking only at Jesus, the originator and perfecter of the faith, who for the joy set before Him endured the cross, despising the shame, and has sat down at the right hand of the throne of God." NASB

We've talked some about specific men and women in the Bible who were flawed, who failed, but who God used mightily when they followed Him. Think of them as part of that "cloud of witnesses." They are testimonials for what God can do in our lives. Knowing that we should be willing to lay aside everything that might hinder us from following Christ. We are to run with endurance. Our eyes are on Jesus.

My stepson participated in cross-country running last year. Cross-country running is different from track running. You run on rough terrain or trails, and you run distance. In his age group, it was usually 2 miles or 5K. There are even special running shoes with spikes so that your shoes can grip the rugged ground. Trust me when I say you cannot be a successful cross-country runner if you are looking backward. In fact, you might just face-plant into the ground or sprain something! That is true of our spiritual race also.

Let's take a look at another passage that tells us why perseverance is so important:

"And not only this, but we also celebrate in our tribulations, knowing that tribulation brings about perseverance; and perseverance, proven character; and proven character, hope; and hope does not disappoint, because the love of God has been poured out within our hearts through the Holy Spirit who was given to us." Romans 5:3-5, NASB

Look at the progression: tribulation brings about perseverance, perseverance brings proven character, proven character brings hope. And hope in Christ never disappoints.

There are so many verses on perseverance, we could create an entire book from their contents. However, I want to close this section with a promise about Christ's perseverance in us:

"For I am confident of this very thing, that He who began a good work among you will complete it by the day of Christ Jesus." Philippians 1:6, NASB

Christ doesn't leave tasks unfinished, and that includes us. If we stay rooted in Him, He will complete the work He has begun in us.

Prayer

We talked about prayer in an earlier chapter, but I want to look more closely at what the Bible says about how to pray and what to pray. There are many resources on the former. The latter is not discussed as much, but the Bible gives us numerous examples from the disciples, the apostles, and Jesus.

First, let's take a look at some of Paul's prayers. When he wrote to the churches and his fellow apostles, he frequently outlined his prayers for them. Sometimes it was a brief mention, such as thanking God for them. Other times he went into great detail about what he prayed for them. We'll start with Ephesians 1:15-19:

For this reason, I too, having heard of the faith in the Lord Jesus which exists among you and your love for all the saints, do not cease giving thanks for you, while making mention of you in my prayers; that the God of our Lord Jesus Christ, the Father of glory, may give you a spirit of wisdom and of revelation in the knowledge of Him. I pray that the eyes of your heart may be enlightened so that you will know what is the hope of His calling, what are the riches of the glory of His inheritance in the saints, and what is the boundless greatness of His power toward us who believe. These are in accordance with the working of the strength of His might." NASB

Paul's prayer to the Ephesians includes several things. First, he gives thanks for them. Paul loved the people of the church in Ephesus (along with all the churches he began and taught). Why is he thankful? He is thankful for their redemption and that they are sealed in Christ. In verse 15 he says, "having heard of the faith in the Lord Jesus that exists among you and your love for all the saints." Paul was thankful for their faithfulness. In other passages, he talks about how the faithfulness of the saints sustained him. I can imagine that as he sat in prison, he recalled to mind the impact churches were having for God's kingdom, and it gave him hope.

He also prayed specifically for their spiritual growth. Paul prayed that God would give them a spirit of wisdom, revelation, and knowledge. He prayed that they would have enlightened hearts and certainty in their calling. Finally, he prayed that they would know deeply the surpassing greatness of God's power in Christ. Paul wanted them to be firm in their faith so they would continue to grow and to spread the gospel.

In Philippians, Paul's prayer is similarly specific. He prays:

- That their love would abound more in knowledge and discernment
- That they would approve the things that are excellent (see also: Philippians 4:8)
- That they would be sincere and blameless
- That they would be filled with the fruit of righteousness

That is an amazing list of things for us to pray for our lives and the lives of our brothers and sisters. For those who we have hurt, I cannot think of better things to pray than for their peace and comfort, for wisdom, for strength, and that they would be rooted in Christ.

Paul goes on in his letters to the Colossians and Thessalonians to thank God for them and to pray that they would be steadfast, that they would grow in wisdom and knowledge, and they would walk in a manner worthy of their calling. I know that is what I want in my own life. I want to know Him more, I want to set my mind on things above, and I want to - from this day forward - walk in a worthy manner.

In the garden, just before Jesus was arrested, He prayed for His disciples and for us. Read with me verses 6-24. I'll just pull out some of Jesus' own words from the passage:

"For the words which You gave me I have given them; and they received them and truly understood that I came forth from You. Keep them in Your name, holy Father, the name which You have given Me, that they may be one as we are one. I do not ask You to take them out of the world, but to keep them from the evil one. Sanctify them in truth. I do not ask on behalf of these alone, but for those also who believe in Me through their word; that they may all be one. I desire that they whom You have given Me be with Me where I am, so that they may see My glory which You have given Me, for You loved Me before the foundation of the world."

That's us. Jesus prayed those things for us! I was browsing social media recently, and apparently, you can pay a celebrity to send a message to a loved one (or yourself) for a birthday or anniversary or some other special occasion. Someone could pay my favorite TV star to tell me Happy Arbor Day. But this is infinitely more awesome. The Savior of the universe prayed to the Creator of the universe on our behalf. What a wonderful Messiah we have.

As believers, when we pray, we have the ultimate eternal Advocate. He wants us to be steadfast. He wants us to be sanctified in truth. He wants us to see His glory. The Bible says the effectual, fervent prayer of a righteous man avails much. Just imagine the fervent prayer of the Son of God!

Perspective

I want to close this chapter by talking a bit about perspective. Merriam-Webster defines perspective as:

> "a mental view or prospect to gain a broader perspective on the international scene the interrelation in which a subject or its parts are mentally viewed places the issues in proper perspective
> also: POINT OF VIEW"
> the capacity to view things in their true relations or relative importance"
> (merriam-webster.com/definition/perspective)

We know our mental and spiritual perspective has a tremendous impact on our lives and actions. And sin certainly skews our perspective. Shame can also twist our perspective, as can fear. But what kind of perspective does Christ want us to have? Colossians 3:2 sums it up well when it says we should set our affection on things about and not on things on the earth. In the gospels, Jesus tells us that where our heart is, there will our treasure be. He is right. The things that are most important to us shape our perspective. It's the reason Christ was so emphatic about the two greatest commandments: Love the Lord your God with all your heart, soul, mind, and strength; and love your neighbor as yourself. These two commandments should outline our priorities and our perspective.

One of the challenges we face is balancing our earthly perspective with our eternal perspective. Yes, we have to pay bills, pay taxes, provide for our families, care for our bodies, and nurture our relationships. However, this life on the present earth lasts less than a century. Eternity is - well - eternal. One of my favorite verses that illustrates this is Romans 8:18:

> "For I consider that the sufferings of this present time are not worthy to be compared with the glory that is to be revealed to us." (NASB)

It's a wonderful verse of hope amid suffering. It's also a great reminder to adjust our perspective. Nothing we experience here on earth - whether hurtful or wonderful - even begins to compare with the glory of eternity.

The Bible talks about the earth having birth pangs waiting for the return of Christ. Labor is painful - I've been through it twice. But once the baby I had longed for was placed in my arms, there was joy. And the pain I endured for a few hours couldn't even compare to the feeling of holding my child. Take a look at what waits for us when the temporary is over:

"Then I saw a new heaven and a new earth...And I saw the holy city, new Jerusalem, coming down out of heaven from God, prepared as a bride adorned for her husband. And I heard a loud voice from the throne, saying, 'Behold, the tabernacle of God is among the people, and He will dwell among them, and they shall be His people, and God Himself will be among them, and He will wipe away every tear from their eyes; and there will no longer be any death; there will no longer be any mourning, or crying, or pain; the first things have passed away...And the throne of God and of the Lamb will be in it, and His bond-servants will serve Him; they will see His face, and His name will be on their foreheads...And there will no longer be any night; and they will not have need of the light of a lamp nor the light of the sun, because the Lord God will illuminate them; and they will reign forever and ever.'"

(Revelation 21-22 excerpts, NASB)

That should absolutely alter our perspectives. Whatever we face, whatever has been, the glory a believer will experience will one day eclipse it all.

My prayer is that as we move forward, pressing on toward the goal, that we will persevere in tribulation, growing in wisdom, and that we would be in ongoing communion with the Father, always interceding. And I pray we will view everything through the lens of God's promise for eternity.

Words from Living Water

1. This week, meditate on Philippians 3:12-14 and James 1:2-5. List the things that God shows you about perseverance and the ways you see Him seeking to build it in your own life and circumstances.

2. Think about a time you have been filled with doubt. Doubt about yourself, about God, or about others. What verses have we discussed in this book (and in particular, this chapter) could you use as a prayer to deal with that doubt?

3. It's hard to have God's perspective sometimes when He sees the big picture and we only see today. Lamentations 3 says "this I recall to mind; therefore, I have hope…" Have there been times in your life in the past where you didn't understand what was going on, but in retrospect, you see how God used that time?

Nave/What Happens After the Well

Chapter 10: Living with Gratitude

As believers who are redeemed, forgiven, and transformed by Christ, we have much to be grateful for every day. Christ not only created the way for us to be reconciled to God, but He also brought us back to fellowship with Him. He has kept His promise to us, His children, just as God kept His promise to Israel. We need to practice gratitude in our daily lives.

When we think of gratitude, we think of thanking someone for what they have done or what they have given. When I am tired from a long day and long commute and come home to folded clothes or takeout provided by my husband, I am grateful. When I receive a gift, I am grateful. But gratitude to God is about more than thanking Him for what He has done. It's about recognizing who He is, how he loves us, and his power and importance in our lives. When I first began discipleship in junior high school, our youth minister used the A.C.T.S. formula for prayer, and that first letter stood for Adoration. That is a good synonym for the gratitude we have toward God.

In that spirit, I want to focus on three aspects of living with gratitude: gratitude for the Nature of God, the Nurturing of God, and the Need for God. We've all got the "thank you for the food" down pat. Exploring these other facets of gratefulness is a great way to increase our understanding of and intimacy with the Father.

Gratitude for the Nature of God

"Who is like You among the gods, LORD? Who is like You, majestic in holiness, Awesome in praises, working wonders?" Exodus 15:11, NASB

God's nature is unfathomable in its entirety. But He has revealed Himself to us through His Word and the person of Jesus Christ. Even the world around us is a testament to God's nature. Here are a few verses that tell us about nature's witness to God's glory:

"The heavens tell of the glory of God;
And their expanse declares the work of His hands."
Psalm 19:1, NASB

"For since the creation of the world His invisible attributes, that is, His eternal power and divine nature, have been clearly perceived, being understood by what has been made, so that they are without excuse." Romans 1:20, NASB

"By faith we understand that the [a]world has been created by the word of God so that what is seen has not been made out of things that are visible." Hebrews 11:3, NASB

"For by Him all things were created, both in the heavens and on earth, visible and invisible, whether thrones, or dominions, or rulers, or authorities—all things have been created through Him and for Him." Colossians 1:16, NASB

God is not just the author and perfecter of our faith, He is the author and perfecter of everything. His nature is imprinted on all of creation, even us, who were created in His image. That is why, whether we acknowledge it or not, we have an innate desire for something - Someone - greater than ourselves. We were made to worship, and all of us do worship something.

When you think of God's nature, what are some words that come to mind? Powerful, loving, holy, patient, wrathful, all-knowing? These are the common terms we often use for God's nature. But there are others. God is creative; we only need to look at the flowers to see that. God is detailed. Look at your own body, from the color of your eyes to the workings of the nervous system, to the unique whorls on each of your fingertips. God is orderly. The distance of our planet from the sun created this livable environment. The moon pushes and pulls the tides with predictability. God is dramatic. Pay attention to the sky the next time there's a spectacular storm. God is also peaceful. Sit outside on a clear summer night, and watch the stars, the fireflies, and the slow passing of clouds. Listen to the babbling of a brook or the sound of summer rain; people buy machines that mimic these sounds to help them relax.

Let's take a look at some other aspects of God's nature.

"The one who does not love does not know God, because God is love." I John 4:8

We talk a lot about love in our society. Our romances typically focus on one type of love, eros, which is sensual or sexual love. Friendship, or phileo, is another type of love we often mention. Overall, in our society, when people proclaim the need to love each other, it is a shallow love. It is a love that is expected to unconditionally endorse, condone, approve of, and agree with whatever the direction of the societal winds happen to be. If you disagree with me, my thinking, or my behavior, you must not love me. You must hate me.

This is not the love of I John 4:8. When it says God is love, it doesn't mean the shallow, unthinking, enabling love that our world demands. In His book, *The Four Loves*, C. S. Lewis expounds on the love of God, the love that should be our aim. It is called agape, and Lewis calls it "charity."

The word charity here does not mean organizations like the Salvation Army or the act of giving money to the homeless man who may be in need, sitting at a corner. This word - agape - is the highest form of love. It is a sacrificial love, it is an unconditional love, and it is a holy love.

Think about the sacrificial love of God. He loved the world so much that He sent His only Son to live sinlessly and then to die for our sin. He knew when His Son was born as a baby that Jesus would suffer, be beaten, be mocked, and be crucified. Jesus Himself loved us with the ultimate sacrifice. Philippians 2 says that Jesus emptied Himself and laid aside His glory. He did this because it was the only way we could be reconciled to God.

"He made Him who knew no sin to be sin in our behalf, so that we might become the righteousness of God in Him." II Corinthians 5:21, NASB

The unconditional love of God is often misunderstood. This is somewhat akin to the love a good parent has for their children. I love my son and daughter unconditionally. There is nothing they can do to remove my love for them or to change the fact that they are my children. But I also want what is best for them. If my child were to rob a bank, I would still love them. But I would not approve of or accept the behavior. As a Christian parent, there is no sin my kids could commit that would cause me to stop loving them, but I will not change my view of sin to fit their comfort. God's love is similar but far greater. God loves His children - those who have surrendered to Christ - unconditionally. No one can snatch us out of His hand. But He does not change His Word for us, and He does not unconditionally accept what He has deemed sin when we choose it.

This is because God's love is holy. He is holy. In his Word, He calls His children to be the same.

"Because it is written: 'You shall be holy, for I am holy.'" I Peter 1:16, NASB

God's love is one with His holiness. This is why He is faithful to chasten His children. This is also why Jesus is the only way, the only truth, and the only life. God cannot share his dominion with sin. His holiness is not compatible with sin. Therefore, in His love, He made a way for us to be reconciled to Him and have our sins forgiven.

In our own lives, every other love must be brought under the subjection of God's agape love. That means our friends, our neighbors, who we are in love with, and how we interact with people must all align with and submit to God and His Word. It's a tall but unchangeable order.

> "Before the mountains were born
> Or You gave birth to the earth and the world,
> Even from everlasting to everlasting, You are God."
> Psalm 90:2, NASB

In Exodus, when God is calling Moses to go to Pharaoh to free the Israelites, Moses asks God, "Who should I say sent me?" God's answer? "Tell them I AM sends you." Later, God says, "I Am that I Am." God is eternal. Before there was anything that we think of as anything, God was. Long after every civilization that currently exists is dust, God will be. It is hard for us to fathom because of our human logic and concept of time. The fact that God has no beginning and no end doesn't make sense to us, which is why many people dismiss it.

I used to watch Star Trek and Dr. Who frequently. Traveling through time and the "space-time continuum" were often themes. The problematic nature of time travel and what happens when one comes back to the present were never quite reconciled in those episodes. For those in my generation, remember *Back to the Future*, when Marty and his siblings began to disappear from the photograph? We see time as linear, and it's almost impossible to think of it any other way.

But God is eternal. It's why He doesn't worry the way we do about timing.

> "But do not let this one fact escape your notice, beloved, that with the Lord one day is like a thousand years, and a thousand years like one day. The Lord is not slow about His promise, as

some count slowness, but is patient toward you, not willing for any to perish, but for all to come to repentance." II Peter 3:8-9, NASB

The above verses, especially verse 9, bring us back to His love. His love is the reason the world is still spinning. He is patiently waiting for those He is drawing to follow Him. However, He doesn't wait forever which is important for us to remember.

> "Lord, You have searched me and known me.
> You know when I sit down and when I get up;
> You understand my thought from far away.
> You scrutinize my path and my lying down,
> And are acquainted with all my ways.
> Even before there is a word on my tongue,
> Behold, Lord, You know it all.
> You have encircled me behind and in front,
> And placed Your hand upon me.
> Such knowledge is too wonderful for me;
> It is too high, I cannot comprehend it."
> Psalm 139:1-4, NASB

God is all-knowing. The fancy word for this is omniscient. He literally knows everything. Like the passage above says, He knows everything about us. This truth bothers some people. They say, "If God controls everything we do, then we're just robots. What's the point?" But knowing something and causing something are two different things.

I'm not sure if it has changed, but it used to be true that no metal of any kind should be placed in a microwave. If I left a spoon in my bowl or covered something with foil and started the microwave, sparks were going to fly. I remember watching someone younger than me try to heat her chocolate milk in the microwave to make hot chocolate. She had stirred the chocolate syrup into the milk, and she placed her glass into the device, spoon and all. I tried to tell her to take the spoon out, but she brushed me off. I knew when she pressed start, there would be fireworks, and she would jump back. That is exactly what happened. Honestly, I also knew when I told her to take out the spoon she wouldn't listen. She was rather stubborn by nature.

I knew what would happen. I knew what she would do. But did I control her? Did I cause the sparks? No. My understanding of her as my friend and the microwave as a device informed me. That is how God is on a vast scale. He knows everything. He created all life. He is omniscient.

Gratitude for the Nurturing of God

Psalm 139 is a good transition place for us to begin talking about God's nurturing of us, for it began before we were even born.

> "For You created my innermost parts;
> You wove me in my mother's womb.
> I will give thanks to You, because I am awesomely and wonderfully made;
> Wonderful are Your works,
> And my soul knows it very well.
> My frame was not hidden from You
> When I was made in secret,
> And skillfully formed in the depths of the earth"
> Psalm 139:13-15, NASB

From the moment our life began, God has been nurturing us physically, mentally, and spiritually. We were formed piece by piece in the image of God. God knew the moment I was conceived that I would have blue eyes, that I would be tall, that my hair would be thick and coarse, and that I would be right-brained and creative.

Psalm 139 speaks extensively about God's physical nurturing of us. Let's take a look at some verses that address God's nurturing of our emotional selves.

> "He heals the brokenhearted
> And binds up their wounds."
> Psalm 147:3

> "He will swallow up death for all time,

And the Lord God will wipe tears away from all faces,
And He will remove the disgrace of His people from all the earth;
For the Lord has spoken."
Isaiah 25:8

I love the phrases, "wipe away tears from all faces" and "remove the disgrace of His people from all the earth." Such hands-on words. In Psalm 56, we read that God keeps all our tears in a bottle. That means He keeps track of every single one, and they are precious to Him. Now, my husband cares if I cry. My friends cry along with me. But no one on earth is so attentive that they keep track of every tear I have ever cried.

"And my God will supply all your needs according to His riches in glory in Christ Jesus." Philippians 4:19, NASB

That word need doesn't just mean food and electricity, though the passage is talking about contentment regardless of circumstances. God knows exactly what we need physically, emotionally, and spiritually, and He can meet all those needs. He is waiting for us to let Him meet those needs in the way that He knows is best. His riches in glory are endless. If God had a bank account, the ledger couldn't contain the number of zeros needed to indicate the balance. As the Bible says, He owns the cattle on a thousand hills. Considering I bought ground sirloin for almost 9.00 a pound a few weeks ago, that is a lot of riches!

When it comes to our spiritual needs, He uses three main avenues to meet and nurture those needs: prayer, God's Word, and fellowship.

"All Scripture is inspired by God and beneficial for teaching, for rebuke, for correction, for training in righteousness." II Timothy 3:16

"For the word of God is living and active, and sharper than any two-edged sword, even penetrating as far as the division of soul and spirit, of both joints and marrow, and able to judge the thoughts and intentions of the heart." Hebrews 4:12, NASB

God gives us everything we need for spiritual knowledge in His completed Word. His words can encourage us, challenge us, correct us, and check our motives. When we study God's Word and strive to be obedient to all of it, we grow stronger spiritually. And that spiritual maturity also benefits our minds and emotions. Sometimes His Word hurts, like an antiseptic on a wound or an injection when we are sick. That pain brings healing.

Several years ago, I was wearing flip-flops in the summer, and my last two toes caught on a curb. Boy, did it hurt. And when I looked down, both toes were pointing in the wrong direction. I pushed them back as best I could and went home. However, when my entire foot began swelling drastically, I decided I might need to go to an urgent care clinic. The doctor called for an x-ray, and sure enough, both were broken. They were also dislocated, and he needed to put them back into place. He told me to hold on and lie back, and he pulled and then rearranged them. If I thought the curb hurt, that toe-pulling just about brought me up off the table. However, the only way they were going to heal properly so that I could walk normally was to be put back into place. That is what God does for us when His Word penetrates our hearts.

"Do not be anxious about anything, but in everything by prayer and pleading with thanksgiving let your requests be made known to God." Philippians 4:6

Our conversations with God reap so many benefits. One of them is relief from worry and fear. God tells us to come to Him with every care we have. In the verse above, He tells us we can come to Him by prayer and pleading and make our requests known. Then, look at what verse 7 says:

"And the peace of God, which surpasses all comprehension, will guard your hearts and minds in Christ Jesus." Philippians 4:7, NASB

Sometimes we may feel as if our prayers are "bouncing off the ceiling." It is hard sometimes to talk to someone we cannot physically see or touch. But God assures us that He hears and that our prayers matter.

"The effectual fervent prayer of a righteous man availeth much." James 5:16b, KJV

Prayer puts us in communication with God. The more we communicate with God, the more we understand His heart and mind. And the more we understand who He is, the more like Him we can become. My dear friend Susan often said, "Prayer doesn't change things for you; it changes you for things." Such wise words! Prayer is one of the ways we become more like God and our desires transform to His desires.

"And let's consider how to encourage one another in love and good deeds, not abandoning our own meeting together, as is the habit of some people, but encouraging one another; and all the more as you see the Day drawing near." Hebrews 10:24-25, NASB

We talked in earlier chapters about the importance of encouraging, challenging, and discipling one another. We talked about how Christ's authentic love compels us to encourage each other to be holy. Verse 24 makes that clear. Verse 25 is also important. It tells us not to neglect meeting together.

I hear a lot of people say, "I love Jesus, but I'm not into organized religion," or "I worship God out in nature, by myself. I'm not into church." Those things sound valid, but they don't align with this verse. Jesus didn't set out alone to fulfill His ministry. He chose 12 men. The early church members didn't take individual nature hikes to worship and grow in their faith. They met together, even if they had to do it in secret. There's nothing wrong with communing with God in nature. I love to go off by myself beside the ocean and pray or worship. But we need fellowship with other believers.

Here's the thing. Churches are made up of human beings, and human beings are imperfect. There is no such thing as a perfect church. Just like families, churches can make mistakes, get off track, even hurt each other's feelings. But God's Word is clear. He doesn't want us to neglect meeting together.

That last phrase, "all the more as you see the Day drawing near," is very important. As the world continues to decline, just as Romans 1 and Jude say it will, we believers will need one another more than ever. We already live in a society that rejects absolutes even as they demand absolute agreement. The closer we get to Christ's return, the more we need to lean on and encourage each other to stay the course.

Gratitude for our Need for God

David wrote psalm after psalm about his need for God. He wrote about needing God's forgiveness, protection, vindication, peace, promises, and strength. We are like David. God made us to need Him, and we should be thankful for that.

But why? In this age where independence is elevated almost to religious status, why is it a good thing to *need* anyone, especially God? Wouldn't it be better if we could just handle everything by ourselves?

The truth is, we can't handle everything ourselves, and when we do, we make a mess. All we have to do is turn on the news to see what happens when we do it our own way. Imagine how different the world might be if everyone embraced their need for God, drew near to Him, and allowed Him to direct their lives. As we have seen, God is a God of order, not chaos. The chaos happens when we leave Him out of the equation.

John 15:15 says is best:

I am the vine, you are the branches; the one who remains in Me, and I in him bears much fruit, for apart from Me you can do nothing. NASB

My father died recently, and people sent flowers. My husband and I ordered an arrangement for the service, and then my mother told me to take it home. I cut the roses, daisies, and baby's breath and created several small arrangements. They were beautiful for about a week. Then the leaves dried, the roses wilted, and the baby's breath began to disintegrate. They weren't connected to anything. The rose bush in my neighbor's yard, however, flourishes for much of the spring and summer. Why? Because the branches and flowers are connected to the main plant - the bush.

When we stay connected to Christ, everything we do flows from Him, and He is the Living Water. As Christians, we might stay on course for a little while on our own, but eventually, we will begin to wilt and dry up, just like the flowers. We need to be connected to Christ

In John 14, Jesus talks about when He will leave His disciples and that He was going to prepare a place for them. He talks about what He has and will show them, and He tells them that He is the way, the truth, and the life. Philip gave this reply:

"Philip said to Him, 'Lord, show us the Father, and it is enough for us.'" John 14:8, NASB

The disciples knew they needed God. They didn't quite understand yet that Jesus *was* God, but they knew they needed the Father.

We've already learned that the psalmist frequently wrote about his need for God. Here are a few examples:

"But I am afflicted and needy;
May the Lord be mindful of me.
You are my help and my savior;
Do not delay, my God."
Psalm 40:17, NASB

"I will raise my eyes to the mountains;
From where will my help come?
My help comes from the Lord,
Who made heaven and earth."
Psalm 121:1-2

David knew that God was the source of all that he needed. He knew the help that God, who made the heavens and the earth, gave him would surpass any other help he could receive. It's one of the things I love about the psalms. The raw, transparent, absolute need for God is so apparent throughout the book.

I am grateful for so many things. I am grateful for salvation. I am grateful for God's patience and long-suffering with me when I rebelled. I am grateful for His conviction and discipline. I am grateful for His Word and His presence. And I am most humbly grateful that He didn't throw me away.

He hasn't thrown you away either. He has plans for you and He created you for a purpose. If you surrender to Him and seek Him above all else, He will use you mightily. That is what He does. And He does it for His glory.

Words from Living Water

1. This week as you go through your day, create a list of the things or people you encounter that/who remind you of the nature of God. Whether it's the glory of His creation in a sunset or His lovingkindness reflected in a friend's care, how many tangible reminders of His nature can you find?

2. In what ways to you most need God's nurturing? Are you grieving and need His comfort? Do you feel unworthy and need His reassurance? Are there things in your life that you are worrying about, and you need his Peace? Go to Him in prayer and ask Him to nurture you through His presence and His Word.

3. It's actually a wonderful thing to need God. He created us for fellowship with Him, so that fact that we need Him is proof of our relationship with Him. In what ways do you need God this week? At the end of the week, reflect on the ways in which He met those needs.

CH 11: Fulfilling Our Calling

"The Spirit of the Lord God is upon me,
Because the Lord anointed me
To bring good news to the humble;
He has sent me to bind up the brokenhearted,
To proclaim release to captives
And freedom to prisoners;
To proclaim the favorable year of the Lord
And the day of vengeance of our God;
To comfort all who mourn,
To grant those who mourn in Zion,
Giving them a garland instead of ashes,
The oil of gladness instead of mourning,
The cloak of praise instead of a disheartened spirit.
So they will be called oaks of righteousness,
The planting of the Lord, that He may be glorified."
Isaiah 61:1-3, NASB

While this passage comes from the book of Isaiah, it has Jesus all over it, as a former pastor of mine would say. Ultimately, this is what He came to do for us through salvation and looking toward eternity. Look at the way Jesus led His disciples and then sent them out. He intended for them - and us - to continue to share the gospel, make disciples, and comfort others with the same comfort that God used to comfort us. So when we are talking about fulfilling our calling, we aren't just talking about being a pastor or evangelist or missionary. We all have a calling, and Isaiah details much of it for us. Let's break it down a bit:

"To bring good news to the afflicted"

The last words or final instructions a person gives are typically considered extremely important. In Matthew 28, after Jesus has risen from the dead and appeared to many, He gives His instructions - His final instructions - before He ascends. These were the last words the disciples would hear Him say.

"And Jesus came up and spoke to them, saying, 'All authority in heaven and on earth has been given to Me. Go, therefore, and make disciples of all the nations, baptizing them in the name of the Father and the Son and the Holy Spirit, teaching them to follow all that I commanded you; and behold, I am with you always, to the end of the age.'"
Matthew 28:18-20

These verses are often referred to as The Great Commission. This is the core of obedience to Christ and fulfilling our calling - sharing the gospel and making disciples. That is His plan for His people.

We've become a bit distracted from this commission by replacing it with things that might - if you really stretch it and squint - be sort of "like" this, but not really. We get caught up in causes, issues, what we are "for" or "against," and how the world "should be." We've forgotten that if we were leading people to Jesus and making disciples, the ills we lament over would abate as lives truly changed. We need to lay aside our temporal, secular attempts at fixing the world and begin again to do it Christ's way.

"He has sent me to bind up the brokenhearted"

I don't know about you, but when I look around, I see a lot of brokenhearted people. On social media, on the news, on the job, and - yes - in church. We see people who are hurting, broken, grieving, and losing hope. I am at the age now where many of my friends are losing their parents. Between the time that I hand-wrote this chapter and typed it into my computer, my own father passed away and is now in Jesus' presence. Over the last year, people I know have lost loved ones, jobs, livelihoods, and their life savings. Children are hurting, relationships are struggling, and the elderly feel forgotten. We are called to comfort each other and bear one another's burdens. We are called to bind up the brokenhearted.

In Matthew 25, Jesus shares what will happen when the Son of Man comes:

"Then the King will say to those on His right, 'Come, you who are blessed of My Father, inherit the kingdom prepared for you from the foundation of the world. For I was hungry, and you gave Me something to eat; I was thirsty, and you gave Me something to drink; I was a stranger, and you invited Me in; naked, and you clothed Me; I was sick, and you visited Me; I was in prison, and you came to Me.' Then the righteous will answer Him, 'Lord, when did we see You hungry, and feed You, or thirsty, and give You something to drink? And when did we see You as a stranger, and invite You in, or naked, and clothe You? And when did we see You sick, or in prison, and come to You?' And the King will answer and say to them, 'Truly I say to you, to the extent that you did it for one of the least of these brothers or sisters of Mine, you did it for Me.'" Matthew 25:34-40, NASB

Binding up the brokenhearted involves empathy, compassion, listening, giving, and serving. We are sensitive to what others need, whether it is a shoulder, a hand to hold, a visit, or - as is customary in the south - a casserole.

"To proclaim the favorable year of the Lord"

In Isaiah 55, the writer states that we should "seek the Lord while He may be found." The opportunity to come to Christ isn't open-ended indefinitely. At some point - and the time is drawing nearer - Jesus will return to claim us. At that point, "the favorable year of the Lord" will be over. Matthew and Luke tell us no one but the Father knows the day or the hour. It will happen in the twinkling of an eye. In addition, there may come a point in someone's life where the Holy Spirit stops drawing. So there should be an urgency in our proclamation.

"To comfort those who mourn"

Before I began typing this chapter, I was on the phone with a dear friend. She's checked on me several times over the past few days following my father's death. I have flowers and a lovely plant in my house sent by friends. Leftover food is in my refrigerator. My husband frequently seems to sense a heaviness in me, and he simply hugs me tightly. These are all examples of people who are doing what Isaiah says - they are comforting those who mourn. This is a very specific type of comfort. When someone we care for is hurting, we sit with them, cry with them, commiserate, and validate their pain. This is part of binding up the brokenhearted, and it is important, but it isn't the end. We want to not only walk alongside someone in their mourning, but we also want to help them to see beyond the temporary and to walk in victory.

If I hold someone's hand and validate their pain, I have given a great comfort. I have acknowledged that yes, this is dark. I have helped them to feel less alone. However, they are still in their pain. The kind of comfort we see here doesn't stop there. In this comfort, we look beyond the mourning to the crown, the victory, the praise. Our comfort - His comfort - directs others toward sufficiency in Christ. As I Thessalonians says, we do not mourn as those who have no hope.

So what is our calling? To share the gospel with urgency. To make disciples as we walk alongside believers. To apply the salve of God's lovingkindness to broken hearts. And, finally, to keep pointing them toward Christ, even amid tribulation. And as for our pasts that Christ has redeemed? Despite our failings, God can use those very experiences and expertise in comfort to comfort others.

I want to close this book with more lyrics/poetry I wrote as I began teaching that ladies' class I mentioned at the beginning - the one I wondered if I was qualified to teach, given my imperfections and past choices. But God reminded me of all those in His Word He redeemed and used. Just like me, they had scars and broken pieces. Broken vessels are His specialty because He gets all the glory when they are still used.

Broken Vessels

Here in the dark
In the quiet moments I can hear the voice
From the past
Telling me the choices I have made
Define me, reminding me

Shame all the shame
And the whispers in my ear
That say He doesn't need me
I was too far gone to ever speak for Him again
But then I felt the wind
From the Lord on high
Saying that's a lie

Chorus
Broken vessels poured the oil on Jesus' feet
Broken spirits are the ones He makes complete
Broken hearts where pride is scattered beneath His wings
He wants to use broken things

I will
Run from the well the share the news of living water and
I'll rise from the sand and step over stones to live
Just like the voice of the man who once denied him I'll
Proclaim to the world all the love He has to give

Chorus
Broken vessels poured the oil on Jesus' feet

*Broken spirits are the ones He makes complete
Broken hearts where pride is scattered beneath His wings
He wants to use broken things*

*And in the quiet if the darkness tries to fall
I'll just remind myself that "Jesus paid at all.....
All to Him I owe"**
*And I can carry light because
He washed me white as snow*

*Quoted lines from "Jesus Paid it All," Public Domain, by Elvina M Hall

About the Author

Laurie Nave is a writer, musician and instructional designer. She lives in Alabama with her husband Larry and a spoiled dachshund named Ginger. In addition, she has two adult children and a teenage stepson.

Laurie grew up in a home where Jesus was taught from a young age. Blessed with godly examples, she wanted to live a life pleasing to Christ. In spite of her failings through the years, God has remained faithful, just as He promises in II Timothy 2:13.

Laurie enjoys writing about God's Word, His faithfulness, and His Great Commission. In addition to writing inspirational books, she enjoys writing suspense, contemporary, and historical fiction. You can follow Laurie's fiction and inspirational writing at: laurienaveauthor.com

Nave/What Happens After the Well

www.ingramcontent.com/pod-product-compliance
Lightning Source LLC
LaVergne TN
LVHW012026060526
838201LV00061B/4476